"It captured the feel of the game so well that I immediately looked up the curling schedule at our local club."

— Sandi Martin, never curled before

"'Hurry hard' and pick up this book — John has summarized curling theory and concepts that will fill the gaps in your curling knowledge as a curling beginner and improver. Grab your broom, put on your grippers, and get ready to be swept off your feet in this introduction to curling."

— Christine Mok, curling improver

"As someone who has helped to develop the Learn to Curl program at Unionville, and has worked with other coaches to teach several hundred people the art of curling, I would highly recommend this book. It delves further into the science and strategy of curling, beyond what can be shared in a few weeks' worth of lessons."

— Kelly Tooley, experienced curler & coach

For my mom,

who when I was 12 gave me

a hand-me-down horsehair brush,

a slip-on slider,

and an escape from hockey.

Curling for Beginners and Improvers

John Robertson

© 2024

CURLING FOR BEGINNERS AND IMPROVERS

John Robertson, PhD

Copyright © 2024 by John Robertson. All rights reserved.

Cover design by John Robertson and Ariadna Villalbi

Photography by Alexis Lindley and John Robertson

Blessed by the Potato Publishing
Toronto, Ontario, Canada
http://holypotato.net

ISBN 978-0-9878189-5-9

Errata: For information and corrections released after the publication of this book please see curlingbeginners.ca. For convenience, links referenced in the text are on the site.

Disclaimer: *Curling is a sport played on ice. Playing involves certain risks, in particular slipping and falling, as well as strains and other injuries. You may need to adapt the suggestions to your own capabilities and risk tolerance. Even when following the best practices, there is a risk of injury or death when playing ice sports, including curling.*

The author cannot be held responsible if you end up loving curling so much that it begins to cause relationship strife, including creating a love of winter and a desire to avoid family vacations during the curling season.

All tips are general guidelines: the author is not **your** *coach and cannot tailor instructions or methods to you, your body's abilities, any injuries you may have, or your current level of play. Please consult an appropriate coach, therapist, kinesiologist, or physician if you require individualized advice or assistance. A book can only ever be a general guide and may not apply to your situation.*

TABLE OF CONTENTS

Introduction 5
The Magic of Curling 7
   Rocks Curling and Contradictions 7
   The Spirit of Curling 7
      Klingon Curling.. 8
      Calling Your Own Fouls... 8
      Rest of On-Ice Etiquette.. 10
      Curling Culture Does Change; Culture is What We Make It 11

The Big Picture 13
   The Game 13
   Scoring... 15
   Teams, Positions, and Duties... 19
   Terminology and Rules... 21

Throwing Rocks 28
   The Physics of the Shot 28
      Equipment and Slipperiness....................................... 31
      Why We Don't Push 33
   Sliding and Balance 34
      Balancing in the Sliding Position 35
      Broom and Stabilizers... 35
      What Happens if You Don't Have Good Balance?... 38
      How to Improve Your Balance 39
      Setup in the Hack.. 41
   Delivery Cadence 42
   Line of Delivery.. 50
   Grip and Release.. 54
   Delivering with a Stick 58

Shot Tolerance 62
Throwing a Hit 64
    Defining Hit Weights 66
    Hitting Which Spot 69
    Generating Hit Weight 70
Your Unique Delivery 71
    No Lift 72
    Flat Foot 74
    Slider Foot Movement 75
    Slider Foot Orientation 76
    Trailing Leg 77
    Broom Placement (for the Slide) 79
    Release Point 80
    Summary 81

Sweeping/Brushing 82
Why we Sweep 82
Keeping a Broom Down 85
Technique 86
    Sweep in Front of the Rock 86
    Clean Strokes 88
    Use the Big Muscles 88
    Open vs Closed 89
    Weight over the broom 93
    Working Together…ish 94
    Skips Stay in the House 95
Communication and Weight Judgement 95
    Playing the Tolerance 98
Directional Sweeping 99
    High Side/Low Side 100
    Approach 1: Scratch Theory 100
    Approach 2: Gradient Theory 102
    Approach 3: Knifing 104
    "Approach" 4: Sweeper Selection 106
    A Quick Directional Sweeping Demonstration 108
    A Reminder for Club Play and In Which I Immediately Contradict Myself 109

Introduction

Playing Together **111**
  Safety 111
  On-Ice Communication 114
  Speed of Play 118
  Staying Out of the Way 119
  Unwritten Rules 120
  Keeping the Ice Clean 125
    Footwear & Grippers 126
    Brooms 127
  Timing Rocks 128

Playing Back End **131**
  The Role of Skip, Vice, and Experience 131
  Standing in the House, Holding the Broom 132
    Setting Line 133
    Being a Target 137
    Calling Line for the Sweepers 138
    Other Duties 141
  Thinking in Curves 141
  Judging the Shot and Making the Sweep Call 148
    Mapping the Ice 150
    Plan B 152
  Scoring, Measurements, Scoreboard 152

Strategy Basics **158**
  Strategy Basics and Ignoring the Pros 158
  Offense and Defense in Curling 160
  Patience and Ignoring Shot Rock 161
  FrESHAIR 164
  Tactics 165
  Shot Selection and the Spooky Centreline 167

Potpourri **172**
  Equipment 172
    Shoes 172
    Grippers 174
    Clothes 174
    Brooms 175
    Delivery Sticks 176

  Other Accessories 177
    Head Protection.. 179
 The Performance Dip 180
 Practice 182
    Finding a Coach 184
 Warming Up Bodies, Cooling Down Sliders............ 186
 Off-Season Training 187
 Soft Skills... 189
 Variant: Doubles.. 191
    Power Play Tips 195
 Happiness and the Zen of Curling......................... 197
 Resources 199

Meta **202**
 A Parting Request: Three Favours 202
 About the Book and Acknowledgements 203
 About the Author.. 205
 About the Photographer 206

Introduction

In storytelling, there are three common conflicts that people try to classify plots into: man vs man*, man vs the environment, and man vs self. Every game of curling is an epic tale containing all three elements, as you try to beat the other team, figure out the ice, and get out of your own head to make your shots.

Curling is a fascinating sport. It can require high levels of athleticism to perform at the top level, blending elements of grace, strength, flexibility, endurance, and strategy into one fascinating – and at times, frustrating – game. It can also be played by people who would not describe themselves with any of those elements, allowing you to bring whatever you have and meeting you there. The inclusiveness makes it one of a small number of sports where multiple generations can play at the same time, and means it can be a hobby you keep up for life.

It is weird, and quirky, and still little-known enough that the increased exposure of the winter Olympics every four years drives noticeable bumps in recruitment to clubs and learn-to-curl events.

And I love it. I have been described as a golden retriever with a favourite toy, trying to show it to everyone who comes near the yard, my eyes full of hope that they understand how much fun it is and that I can help bring joy to their lives too if they would just give it a try. I hope I can help you discover the allure of curling, and that you,

---

* Please forgive the anachronism, but updating it to read "person vs person" didn't seem to be the right poetry for an opening line.

dear reader, may be one of many more people who will go out and try curling, work to get better at curling, and find joy in it.

This book is intended to be full of tips and how-tos for the beginner curler and those looking to improve, and is hopefully enough fun to read that even experienced curlers will find it worth their time. It is not intended to be the sole remaining relic of the sport in a far-distant post-apocalyptic world, so I won't start with a history of Scots throwing rocks on lochs or the exact dimensions needed to build your own sheet of ice. My apologies to the survivors of the zombie/robot/alien uprising if you are trying to rebuild society curling-first (*i.e., correctly*) and were hoping to use this book as a reference.

Anyway, as a reader, you can expect some irreverent non sequiturs and jokes along the way, along with some tips and explanations of why we want a certain form or approach. As an athlete trying to learn curling, you can expect that there will be ups and downs in your performance: even with steady objective performance, you'll start to feel let down by your draw weight or hitting when your strategy starts calling for more and more precision once you know you can make certain shots. As a person, you can expect to find a new hobby that you'll hopefully love as much as I do, and will help keep you physically and socially fit for a long time to come.

THE MAGIC OF CURLING

ROCKS CURLING AND CONTRADICTIONS

Curling is a magical and special sport.

It is full of contradictions and juxtapositions that give it its unique charm.

We are hurling forty-pound rocks across a hundred feet of ice, with a precision of inches. Despite the mass and momentum of a hunk of granite sliding on ice, the sport is so finely tuned that the heating from rubbing a piece of fabric on the ice makes a significant difference to the ultimate trajectory. A rock that could take down an unsuspecting person can be ruined by a stray hair.

The way the rocks move down the ice – the curl itself – is surprisingly poorly understood by physics. If after your curling match, you find yourself at a bar in a heated discussion and attempt to re-create a shot by sliding a wet glass on a tabletop, you'll find that it curls in the *opposite direction* of what the rock did on the ice.

It's a sport filled with yelling – so very much yelling! – and yet none of it mean-spirited or in anger. We yell to encourage our teammates, and keep quiet to respect our opposition. This magical set of contradictions and attitude to the sport is often summed up as "the Spirit of Curling."

THE SPIRIT OF CURLING

Every group of humans creates its own culture, full of unwritten rules. I'm not just talking about countries, like how tipping is an essential part of dining out in Canada and the US, but not done in Japan. Even within Canada, culture varies quite a bit in certain ways from province to province, or even within areas of a large city like Toronto.

Curling has a different culture than a lot of other sports, and that particular culture largely gets labelled "The Spirit of Curling," and while labels can be helpful... that one isn't exactly self-explanatory, so let's break it down a bit.

Klingon Curling

In Star Trek, one of the fictional species of humanoids that the crew of the Enterprise encounter a lot are the Klingons, a group of warriors with a keenly developed sense of honour. While they may get their blood up and seek victory on the field of battle in the name of Kahless, it may equally be "a good day to die." There is no dishonour in losing to a superior foe. As long as you fight with honour, you will find your place in *Sto'vo'kor*.

And so it is with curling. We try to win, read incredibly long and convoluted emails to try to squeeze out a nugget of wisdom to improve our game, show up ready to play, and maybe even book practice ice to get better. But at the end of the day it's no big deal if we lose, as long as we tried our best and put in a good game.

What it really boils down to for each end in a game is being able to answer *yes* to the question: did I bring honour to the end? That's a big part of The Spirit of Curling.

Qapla.

Calling Your Own Fouls

Along with that is this notion that we call our own fouls, and we throw ourselves upon the mercy of our opponents.

The Magic of Curling

Then, in turn, it is incumbent upon our opponents to not take advantage – the two most common remedies for a burned stone are to leave it where it ended up (or put it back if it was a stationary stone that was moved), or to put it where you *reasonably* thought it was going to end up without the burn. (There is also the option of taking it out of play and returning everything to where it was before the shot – this is more often considered the nuclear option and rarely used.)

Here is how important that idea is: in other sports, it is accepted and common to use fouls and out-of-bounds tactically. In basketball, if you want to stop the momentum of a play, you may purposefully throw a ball out of bounds, or try to make contact with a player and then fall in a certain way to make it a foul on them*. Soccer is infamous for players acting hurt (they even have a term for it: "diving") after even minor accidental collisions to try to get penalty shots against the other team.

In curling, if you see that *whoops*, your team's shot is heading for something very bad (like taking out your own rock or promoting an opposing stone), you may be tempted to burn it and take it out of play. This is so anathema to curling that it has one of the most severe punishments: if you purposefully burn your stone, you instantly lose the game. Not "oh, let's put it where we think it would have gone," no, it's game over, go home, goodbye – we do not play with people who do not bring honour to The Sprit of Curling.

---

* Aside: that drove me insane as a kid – we had learned that basketball was a *non-contact sport*, but you'd never know it watching the pros or the way a lot of guys in a casual university 3-on-3 league acted (apparently the Americans gave up and it's now classified as a contact sport).

And it's so anathema, it's not even in the rulebook – I went to try to find a link to include, but there isn't a specific numbered rule to cite that I could find. Yet somehow I *know* that is the appropriate answer for that case that has never happened to me in two decades of curling. Instead, intentionally burning a stone to avoid a bad outcome just falls under the general category of "hey, that's cheating, and against The Spirit of Curling, so we're done here." Indeed, those parts are right at the beginning of the rulebook*, before any numbered rules: *"I will conduct myself in an honourable manner both on and off the ice; I will never knowingly break a rule."*

Anyway, even within that, there are unwritten understandings in different leagues. In our competitive mixed doubles league, I had thrown a peach of a shot, and in-between the hog lines had accidentally touched the rock – just barely grazed it with my broom. There was no way that touch was going to affect the stone's outcome, but a touch – any touch – between the hog lines means the rock comes off so I pulled it. That same touch in our tag league or recreational mixed league would likely not see us actually pull the rock off – we'd tell the other team what happened, the other Skip would wave and laugh, and it would be fine. With so many new curlers in those leagues just finding their coordination, we'd have precious few rocks left in play if we pulled every one that had a minor tick from a broom.

Rest of On-Ice Etiquette

There are lots of other elements that go into the Spirit of Curling, and general on-ice etiquette, which we will get back to closer to the end of the book. The main one to mention up front is:

---

* Curling Canada *Rules of Curling for General Play* 2022–2026, p4.

We play other people not "the opposition." Every game begins and ends with a handshake (or post-covid, a fist-bump, or an awkward half-handshake half-fist-bump half-giggle). Our opponents are our friends (and in some leagues, potential future teammates). While we want to bring a good game and, hopefully, win, it's still friendly and we still respect them as people. They are not a faceless "opposing force" to try to wipe off the map.

Curling Culture Does Change; Culture is What We Make It

Culture is an emergent phenomenon. There are ways to codify parts of it, but that can only ever have so much success – the Académie Française and Bill 101 can work hard to prevent catchy English words and phrases from making their way into the speech of the French. However, their efforts can't stop them all if the French-speaking people happen to find English words catchy or useful.

Culture is really all about how most of us interact with others. What we consider "normal" and allow to be considered "acceptable" (or "unacceptable") is a big part of what makes up culture.

So curling culture is just all of us and how we choose to play with one another, how we hang out and treat each other before and after the games. And that can change based on what we do going forward, how the next generation thinks and changes. What we do right now, and in all the future moments before us decides what the culture will be.

It can change unintentionally: if we get too competitive in our games, and forget about bringing honour to each end, we may not call those fouls on our own. Or we may stop being outraged when a team responds to an infraction with the full force of what the rules allow instead of the spirit in which they should be interpreted.

It can change with intention and purpose, too: if any parts of curling culture aren't suiting us, we can jettison them. Drinking and driving used to be more permissible and often overlooked, but I don't think any one of you reading this would let someone across the table from you pound back four beers then stumble out behind the wheel, it's just no longer within the acceptable window of behaviour.

Being welcoming is, increasingly, an important part of curling culture. There are corners of the sport where performance is important – nobody is calling me up to join their team to make a run at the Brier or Mixed Nationals because I'm not that good and performance matters there. But at the club level, we want you here, regardless of any of those factors. *You* belong here. Even if you can't get down into a slide at all, we can find a way to modify the game to include you, such as using a standing delivery with a stick. Just come out and have fun with us: the process is more important than the result.

That goes for other elements of being welcoming. Curling has historically been, to use the technical term, "super-duper white." But hopefully today anyone can find a welcoming smile when they come try the sport (and that as a community, curlers all over will continue to improve in being welcoming to all).

And perhaps this book will help those starting a new team or club. In addition to learning the technical skills to deliver a rock, it's highly important to build a positive, welcoming culture.

THE BIG PICTURE

THE GAME

Curling is a game of skill and strategy played on ice. Teams take turns sliding granite stones toward a target over 100 feet away. The rocks can bump other rocks out of the way as an end progresses, until all rocks have been thrown, at which point the team with the rock closest to the centre (within 6') score.

Teams are typically four members, throwing a total of eight stones (i.e., two each), though there are variants, in particular Mixed Doubles (more on that much later – for the rest of this intro we will stick to traditional four-person curling).

The stones are fairly heavy, about* 42 lbs. However, they are not lifted, just slid across the slippery ice, which makes the feat of sending them down over 100' of ice possible.

The† really cool thing about curling is the **curl** itself: the rocks do *not* travel in straight lines. This curved path is where the game gets its name from. And it is *magic* – not

---

* There's a lot of "about" in the descriptions of curling dimensions. There is wiggle room provided in the rules, so rinks can be built with slightly varying dimensions and still be regulation. The stones usually start at ~44 lbs (the maximum allowed size), but material is slowly lost as they are resurfaced, and can still be used in play down to 38 lbs (the minimum allowed size).
† As if I could pick just *one* really cool thing about curling.

just in the sense of "I feel awe and wonder watching its beauty," but in the "physics doesn't have a widely agreed upon mechanistic basis for why they move that way".

It means that you can put up a rock in front of the target (which we call a "house") to act as a guard, and if you throw another just right, it will curve around that guard and sit behind it. The curl depends on how fast the rocks are moving, so a faster throw to try to remove the stone sitting in the house behind the guard may not curl enough to make contact, opening up a number of cool strategic possibilities.

The magical curl is enabled in part by how special the ice surface is: it is "pebbled" with tiny droplets of water that freeze on top, producing a texture to the ice. That makes it easier for players to stand on it with soft rubber grippers providing traction, and affects how the rocks travel over it.

The rocks are also pretty special: modern rocks are usually made of two kinds of granite, a slug of material to run on the ice inserted inside a larger torus that's used as an outer layer to bang into other rocks. And the granite comes from just two quarries (even the rocks manufactured in Canada) – Ailsa Craig in Scotland and Trefor in Wales.

In the game of curling, teams are sliding (we use the verb "throwing" though the stones should stay on the ice, "delivering" also works) rocks from one end to the other, by sliding in a deep lunge with the rock for a short while to set it on the correct trajectory before letting it go. Then the team's sweepers can use fabric brushes to clean the ice (even a tiny hair can change the path the rock takes!)

The Big Picture

and change the properties* of the ice, to influence the final shot.

Lots of strategy goes into deciding which shots to attempt: getting your rocks closest to the centre of the house (called "the button") gets you points, but the other team can throw shots to take your rocks out of play, so having some in the non-scoring area in front of the house as guards may be prudent. And you may need to call some take-outs of your own to create some space to score or prevent the other team from scoring.

The game is divided up into "ends", where an end is a cycle of throwing all 16 rocks (8 per team) to the scoring end, then determining the score. Then a new end starts, the teams throw the rocks back the other way to the other house on the sheet, and determine the score again. A "typical" game is nominally 8 ends, though professional games may be 10, and in recreational clubs time may be a factor limiting play to fewer ends (e.g., up to 8 or however many the teams can fit in 2 hours, whichever comes first).

SCORING

Scoring is *pretty* simple in curling: the team whose rock is closest to the middle scores. And the scoring team gets more points for each rock that they have closer to the middle than the opponent team's closest.

So only one team can score in an end.

The rings look like bullseyes from things like archery, but the different rings and colours mean *nothing*, they merely

---

* Are they polishing the ice, heating it, scratching it? A bit of all the above. Which one matters for affecting the curl? Science is still working to answer that question – *magic*!

serve as a visual aid to help determine which rock is closer — a rock barely touching the outside is worth one point, just like one that's right on the pinhole in the middle: one point per rock that's closer than the opponent's closest.

Teams take turns throwing rocks one at a time (so Team A throws one, then Team B throws one, then Team A throws their second, then Team B throws their second). This means one team gets to throw second, and more importantly, their last rock will be the last rock of the end. This is called having **hammer** (or last stone advantage), which is considered an advantage.

If the team without hammer * scores, it is called "**stealing**" (or a "stolen end" or "a steal").

After a team scores in an end, they will then throw first the next end, giving the other team hammer. So the lowest score you can give up to get hammer back is 1, and is considered a minor victory. Thus holding the hammer team to 1 also gets a special name and is called "**forcing**" (or "a force").

Different venues can use different scoreboards for displaying the score. Some have electronic scoreboards that resemble a spreadsheet, or a baseball scoreboard. However, the traditional curling club scoreboard looks like this:

---

* I am surprised that curling still hasn't come up with a cutesy name for the team without hammer, instead defining it as the absence of the hammer and using all those words to do it. Just in case this book does well enough to change the culture, let's try a name on for size: the {insert name here} team. Oh no, I couldn't come up with a catchy name either! [Ed note: *Nail* is right there, John]

The Big Picture

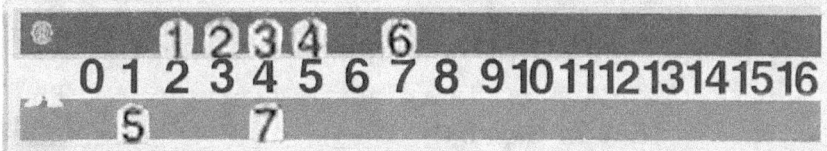

It has numbers to represent the points across the middle, and a zone at the top and bottom for each team (in this picture, blue at the top, red at the bottom, or black and grey if you're reading on a black and white device or the print edition*). In those zones, you hang cards ("tags") for each end, with the number on the tag representing the end that was played.

So to read it, you scan across the numbers in the middle, and the furthest right that has a tag is how many points that team has in total. In the above image, the blue (or black, top) team has 7 points, and the red (or lighter grey, bottom) team has 4 points. That's because the furthest-right tag for blue (top) is the [6] tag, above the 7 in the middle for points, and the furthest-right tag for red (bottom) is the [7] tag, below the 4 in the points row.

You can read the history of the game by looking at the jumps between tags. They got those points by blue scoring 2 in the first end (the [1] tag is above the points for 2), 1 in the second end (the [2] tag is above the points for a total of 3, showing that they had one more than the prior tag), 1 in the third end, 1 in the fourth end, and 2 in the sixth end, for a total of 7 points. Red scored 1 in the fifth end and 3 in the fourth end, for a total of 4 points.

For some people, this style of scoreboard looks a little backwards – baseball, by way of contrast, has the ends

---

* A quick note on Photoshop: we have retouched some images to make them clearer when displayed in black & white. For those with colour devices, the reds will often appear unnaturally bright. Which leads to a second-level footnote: red & blue are very traditional curling colours, and *lousy* choices for colourblind players.

17

(or "innings" as they call them) across the grid, and then tags for the points. In part that's needed because in baseball both teams can earn points every inning. That also means that in baseball you need a whole bunch of each kind of card – 18 cards with 0s on them, 18 cards with 1s on them, 18 with 2s, etc.

For curling, because only one team can score each end, we only need one tag per end with this style. And the tags always come out in the order the ends are played in – you don't have to rummage through a bin of them to find the score you need. If the game before you properly cleaned up and put the tags in order, the [1] tag is at the front of the pile ready for you after you play the first end, and the [2] tag right behind it. You can see the little pocket with fresh tags just peeking out in the bottom-left corner of the scoreboard, left of the zero.

It's also possible for neither team to score in an end. This is called a "blank" end. In regular curling, a blank means the team with hammer (last rock advantage) keeps it going into the next end (in a variant of curling called doubles, the hammer switches teams on a blank). Often there is a 0 or a spot for "blank" ends on a scoreboard where the end tags can be put up (usually on the team keeping hammer's row). In rare cases, you can stack the end cards on top of the prior score. At our club, there is a single peg for each team under the 0. If there's more than one blank end, we'll start putting the cards under the 16 (and the 15, etc.) – we're pretty good at understanding when that's being used as a placeholder for a blank end versus when someone has legitimately racked up a score that high.

Finally, the justification for why traditional curling scoreboards are laid out this way has to do with reducing the number of tags needed. With two pages of explanation on how to read it, it's clearly not because it is intuitive.

For televised events with electronic scoreboards, something closer to a baseball scoreboard layout is typically used.

Teams, Positions, and Duties

In traditional curling, teams are composed of 4 players:

- The Lead
- The Second
- The Vice*
- The Skip

The Lead throws the first two rocks for the team, the Second the next two, the Vice the next two, and the Skip the final two. Collectively, the Lead and Second are sometimes called "the front end" while the Vice and Skip together are called "the back end."

When they are not taking their turns to throw rocks, players are serving as sweepers for their team's rocks, with two exceptions. The Skip will be standing at the other end of the sheet (the side with the scoring house), calling the shots and deciding on the strategy, and holding their broom to act as a target for the throwers. There are situations where the Skip will sweep, but they're starting the shot at the other end of the ice from the throwers and sweepers. The other exception is the Vice, who will sweep for the Lead and Second shots, but when the Skip goes to throw, the Vice goes into the house to hold the broom as a target.

The sweepers (two of the Lead, Second, and/or Vice depending on who is throwing) will start at the delivery end with the thrower, and follow the rock down the sheet,

---

* There are several variations on the name for the third player, including "Third", "Vice-Skip", and "Mate". I'll stick with "Vice".

sweeping as needed (which they may determine on their own accord, or they may be told to do so by the Skip or Vice in the house).

Which brings us to the duties on a team: there is one player in charge of the house*. This player is typically the Skip, or the Vice during the Skip's shots, and is calling the strategy. The person in the house is also allowed to sweep their own rocks during the opponent's turn, or the opponent's rocks but only after they cross the T-line (the line running across the middle of the house).

That leaves one person as the thrower and the remaining two as sweepers. The thrower's duty is to deliver the rock and be sure that they let go before sliding to the hog line on the delivery end. The sweepers' duty is to sweep when needed and communicate with the person in the house about the speed ("weight") of the shot.

For safety's sake, everyone is empowered to stop a rock before it goes flying out of play (outside the sidelines on the sheet or through the backline), to prevent rocks from interfering with play on other sheets or hitting someone.

Finally, the Vice will often have the remaining jobs that pop up: taking the coin toss for hammer before the game, agreeing with the other team what the score is (i.e., which rock(s) are closer than others), putting the score on the scoreboard, and reporting the score to the league/tournament scorekeeper after the game.

---

* There are *two* sets of rings or "houses" painted on the sheet, but when we say "the house" we mean the one at the scoring end, not the delivery end.

TERMINOLOGY AND RULES

The rulebook exists, and I don't want to bore you with all the rules, but I suppose a proper introduction can't be made without covering at least the major ones. Likewise, I shouldn't assume that you already know (or will look up) all the terms that will get thrown at you in this book.

Stone, rock: the big (38-44 lbs) hunk of granite we play the game with. A stone has a small ring on the bottom that actually makes contact with the ice (the "running band"), which is typically an insert of a different type of granite, and a wider "striking band". A handle on top is used to hold it for delivery and usually is coloured to indicate which team the rock belongs to.

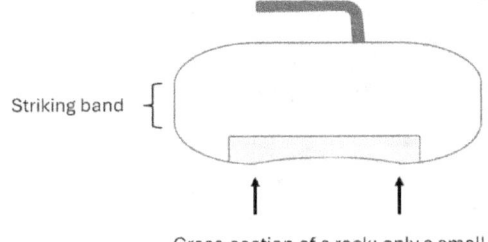

Cross-section of a rock: only a small ring makes contact with the ice (the "running band"), the rest of the bottom curves up in a concave dish shape. An insert of a different kind of granite is often used for the running surface (shaded in cross-section).

Bottom view: Arrows highlight running band

Broom, brush: the stick with a fabric-covered head you use to sweep (or brush*).

Sheet: The long segment of ice a game is played on. A club or arena typically will have several sheets of ice.

---

* Or mop? The household chore that most resembles the movements in curling is mopping, but sweeping is the more traditional verb, while brushing is gaining popularity.

Each sheet will have a house and hacks at both ends, with play alternating directions in each "end" of play.

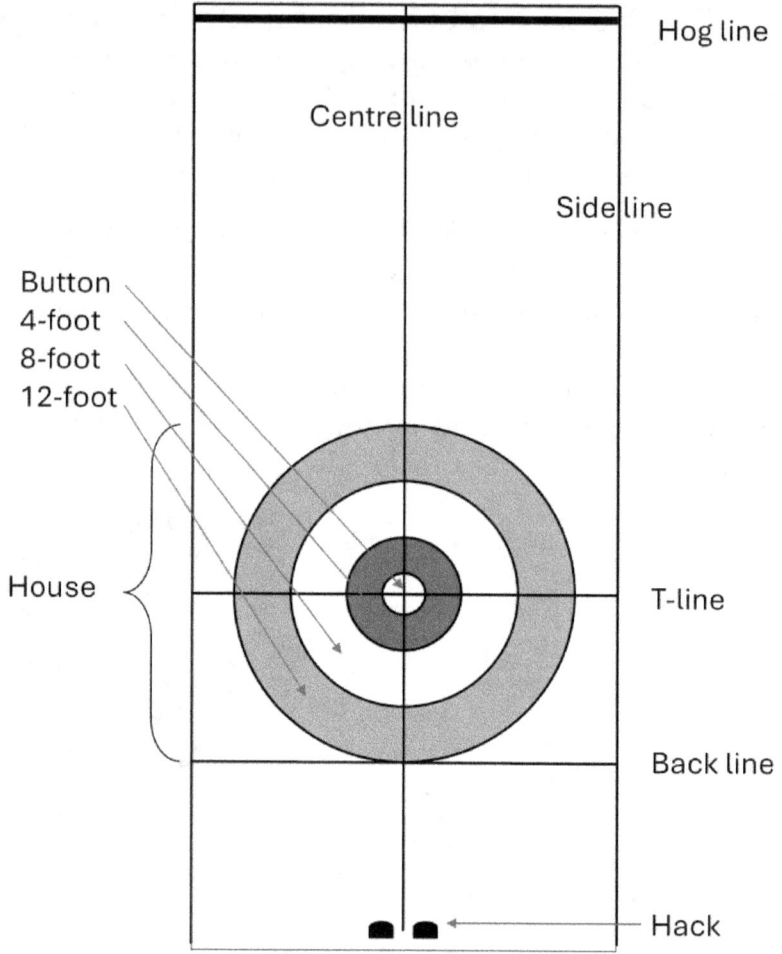

House: the 6' radius (12' diameter) set of rings painted on the ice that serve as the scoring area. There is one painted on each side of the sheet, but when we say "the" house, we're referring to the one you are throwing toward in that end to score in. Sometimes called "**the paint**" when referring to the scoring area.

Button: The smallest circle in the house, with the "pin" in the centre of it.

Pin: The pin is a small hole in the ice located in the very centre of the house, where the T-line and centreline intersect. The hole can be used to anchor a measuring device, and the pin is defined as the true centre of the house: the circles painted or drawn may not be perfectly circular or perfectly centred, so when rocks are close it is the measurement of the inside edge to the pin that counts.

4-foot/8-foot/12-foot: Each concentric circle in the house, the measurement refers to the ring's outer diameter. The "top" 4-foot/8-foot/12-foot (or "top house" more generally) refers to the portion of that ring "above" or "in front" of the T-line, which is the part closer to the hog line/where the guards are. The "back" 4-foot/8-foot/12-foot refers to the part behind the T-line, closer to the backline/boards.

Hack: A pair of sloped rubber blocks inserted in the ice that deliveries start from.

Touching a line/Crossing a line: Curling rocks have a small "running band" that actually touches the ice, which is smaller than the outer diameter of the rock. For rules involving whether a rock "touches" a line, there's no actual physical contact involved: it's the outer edge of the stone (the widest part of its striking band) that counts, when viewed directly from above (or at the appropriate angle, such as aligned with the sideline or hog line).

Hog line: A thick line 21' in front of the centre of the house. On the scoring side, rocks must *fully* cross the hog line to be in play (rocks that stop short are removed from play), with the exception of rocks that strike other rocks already in play*. On the delivery side, the thrower must release before the rock *touches* the hog line.

T-line: A line crossing through the middle of the house, across the narrow dimension of the sheet. The person in charge of the house (usually the Skip) may sweep the other team's rocks after they cross the T-line. When sweeping your own rocks, only one member of your team may keep sweeping after the T-line (in part, think of this rule as creating space for the other team's Skip to be able to sweep your rock).

A second rule related to the T-line is on the delivery end: a player may stop and reset their delivery if they stop before the rock reaches the near T-line (in practice this most often occurs because the player fell pushing out of the hack or forgot to take their gripper off and didn't move very far attempting to slide).

Backline: A line behind the house. Rocks *fully* crossing this line are out of play.

Sideline: A line up either side of the sheet. Rocks *touching* the sideline are instantly out of play. In some cases (particularly for the sheets at the side of the arena), there is a board or physical bumper that serves as the sideline, in which case a rock touching the side (and thus leaving play) may be more clear.

Centreline: A line running the length of the sheet up the centre. For most play, the line is a visual guide only,

---

* The shorthand version of this rule ("a rock has to fully cross the hog line to be in play") is often taught in learn-to-curl or what is remembered by players because it's pretty rare that the other situations happen: a rock stops over the hog line but close enough to it that if a second rock then strikes it, that second rock will be touching the hog line (or fully on the wrong side of it). If this happens several times, each rock that is "in play" from this rule is also "in play" to be struck in turn.

however at the pro level a new rule was recently introduced that prevents guards from being "ticked" off of the centreline in the first five rocks of an end. This rule may eventually be implemented in recreational play, so be aware of it and the rules for your league.

Boards: Behind the playing area of the ice sheet is an area raised above the ice, typically carpeted, called the boards.

Guard: A rock in play (i.e., over the hog line) and in front of the house (i.e., not touching the paint or scoring area). Also the term for the shot to end up with a guard.

Free guard zone: A rule that you cannot hit the other team's guard out of play in the first 5* shots of the end (i.e., the hammer team's Second is the first one permitted to take out a guard). You are generally allowed to hit your own guards out of play. You are allowed to move an opponent's guard, as long as it stays in play (including into the house, where it can then be hit out of play on any subsequent shot). Note however that a "**no tick rule**" has recently been implemented for guards on the centreline in national and international competitions, and may in the future be used in recreational leagues.

Draw: A shot that aims to put a rock in play in the house.

Tap, tick: A shot that aims to make contact with and move a rock in play, but not take it out of play.

Raise: A kind of tap that aims to move a rock in play, typically referring to moving it closer to the scoring area.

Freeze: A draw that aims to stop just short of or gently touching a rock in play, to end up very close to it.

---

* It is often explicitly called the "5-rock free guard zone" because the rule has evolved over the years from a 3- and 4-rock version.

Hit, take-out: A shot that is thrown faster with the aim of having the thrown rock make contact with and then take another rock out of play.

Double: A take-out that aims to take two rocks out of play.

Backing: A rock that can serve as the target for another rock to freeze to. Having backing means it can be more difficult to hit a rock out of play, as the target rock will in turn (likely) hit the backing.

Weight: Not weight at all, but the speed of a rock. Terminology chosen specifically to drive physicists mad.

Pick: When a piece of debris (often invisible and only known by its effects on the rock, such as a hair) affects the trajectory of a rock. The sudden unexplained slow-downs or turns in a rock are from "picks" or the rock is said to have "picked."

Burn: If a player accidentally touches a rock in motion (e.g., with a body part or their broom), it is *burned*. The remedy depends on when the interference happened. Between the two hog lines the rock should be immediately removed from play (including if the thrower holds on past the hog line). If it occurs after the scoring end hog line, the shot is allowed to play out. The non-offending team may choose* to allow things to stay as they are (ignore the burn), move rocks to where they reasonably thought they would have ended up, or reset rocks to where they were before the throw and take the offending rock out of play.

---

* In recreational leagues we're often forgiving and let the rocks stay where they end up, or make small adjustments we think will get the result that would have occurred without the burn – though another reason to prefer those options is that it can be hard to remember where the rocks were without an instant replay.

Hammer: Having last-rock advantage.

Force: When the team with hammer only scores a single point.

Steal: When the team without hammer scores.

Blank: When nobody scores (i.e., no rocks are touching the house at the conclusion of an end). The hammer team will retain the hammer.

Turn, handle, spin: These are different words used to refer to the rotation of the rock. As we let go of the rock in the delivery we "apply a handle" or "put on a turn." When setting up the shot, we may choose one turn over the other. The more objective description for which turn to use is clockwise/counter-clockwise, but from the outside or inside may be used (where it's assumed that the listener knows which turn corresponds to each direction for the proposed shot), or "in-turn" and "out-turn". A rock may have more or less spin, usually measured by the number of rotations it makes down a full sheet of ice.

In-turn, out-turn: Ways to describe whether the rock has a clockwise or counter-clockwise rotation applied. The origin is that when releasing a rock, one way would naturally make your elbow turn in, the other out – for a right-handed thrower a clockwise rotation would be an in-turn. Quite commonly used, particularly by TV commentators, however we are trying to discourage its use as the meaning of in-turn or out-turn is opposite for left-handed vs right-handed curlers (leading to fun clarifications such as "my in-turn or your in-turn?").

THROWING ROCKS

THE PHYSICS OF THE SHOT

From a physics perspective, a shot is defined by three parameters in your control: the direction, speed, and rotation (then once out of your hand, all the stuff related to the ice, but that's a whole other topic).

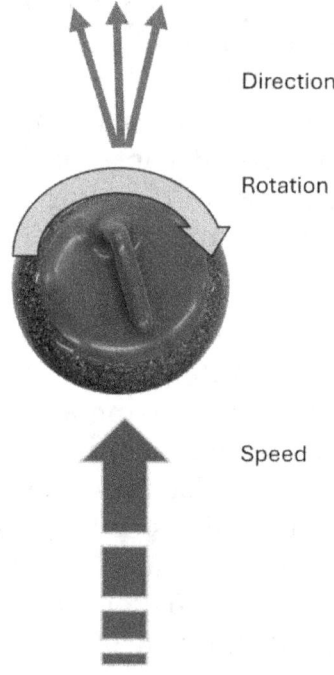

By separating out how each component of the shot is applied to the rock, we can get more precise control over how we send that big hunk of granite hurtling down the long sheet of ice.

Throwing Rocks

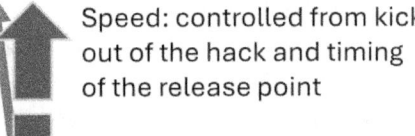

Speed: controlled from kick out of the hack and timing of the release point

Rotation: clean spin around the rock's centre, does not take the rock off the line

Line of delivery: set from the set-up and kick out of the hack, held through to release, rock is on a line right to the skip's broom

The rotation is perhaps the easiest to get right consistently: we start the rock with the handle turned to point at 10 or 2 o'clock*, and turn to 12 as we let go. As long as you know to do that every time, and you set up your handle right as you're getting ready to deliver, it's automatic. You don't even think about the rotation as you release, just turn it to 12 o'clock to give it a nice spin, without "setting it out" or "getting it started."

Those terms refer to getting the rock off the line of delivery as you're adding the rotation. The goal is to spin it cleanly around the rock's centre, independent of the line. If you do push it off the line while adding the spin, that's setting it out, and if you nudge it inside the line that's getting it started/dumping it (it appears to start curling early).

---

* Gen Z/Alpha readers who are confused at this terminology are encouraged to do an internet search for "clock face directions."

The line (direction) is also partly taken care of in set-up: we point everything to the target (Skip's broom), slide* straight to the broom, and release still aiming right at the broom. It requires a bit more thought and focus: keeping your eyes up at the broom, making sure your slide is true, making minute adjustments as needed.

The traditional curling slide is not merely a form that we follow because it's what we do in the sport and for the challenge of it, it also allows us to use different muscle groups to try to take control over each of the parameters of the shot.

Line can be something you get pretty close to accurate the vast majority of the time. Good technique should see you lining up to the Skip's broom (or other target in practice sessions) as you get set in the hack, going to the target along every part of the pull-back and slide, and keeping your focus on that target.

Then there's the speed (or weight as we curlers call it, I'm convinced specifically to drive physicists mad). That is, in my opinion, the hardest part. It's in large part a matter of art and feeling, and after 20-some years of curling I still give up points by blasting a draw that "just has to touch paint" right through or coming up short of the house. So I obviously can't tell you how to find the right weight, but I can talk a bit about what's happening to get there.

Most of the weight is going to come from your push out of the hack (your leg drive/kick and the cadence of dropping your hips/pressing forward). Some people will add or remove a tiny bit with a small arm extension/pull-back.

---

* You can curl without being able to slide: with the use of a delivery stick, you can deliver a stone from an upright position. We'll get into the mechanics of that in a few chapters, but many of the underlying principles are going to be the same, including moving straight to the target, putting on a clean rotation, etc.

But to a large extent, let's just say that all of the weight comes from the push out of the hack.

That means that after you kick out of the hack, the only thing that's happening is the rock (and you) are decelerating (slowing down) through the slide. So you kick out to try to get a bit above the final speed needed, slide for a bit to make sure you're on the line, then as you slow down to the point where the weight feels right (and I know of no systematic approach here other than practice and feel), you put a nice clean rotation on the rock and let it go.

Some of us you'll see slide almost to the hog line before letting go, but if you're losing speed fast, then you should be letting go sooner, when you and the rock are at the right speed for the shot. There is no universal "right" spot to release the rock. There are no bonus points for sliding all the way to the hog line first. It's whenever you feel you're at the right speed for the shot... which is disappointing because I wish there was a more systematic way to get the weight right. If you're coming up light a lot, you may have to let the rock go a little sooner than you want to if that's the point in your slide when you're hitting the weight.

Anyway, keep these basic principles in mind as we go through the steps of the traditional "Curling Canada" delivery, and how we build up to a delivery with precise control over each of the three important parameters of the shot.

Equipment and Slipperiness

There are many factors that can affect what your deceleration looks like. If you're using tape on your shoe, that's slippery, but not all *that* slippery. If you have a rubber gripper on your non-sliding foot, that's going to be grabbing the ice and dragging you down very quickly. So you'll find that you have to kick fairly hard, and then you'll slow down fast, and the window of your slide when you're actually at the right point for the called shot is fairly small. Conversely, a thick Teflon slider and a toe dip on your trailing foot will help you slide with less friction, maintaining your speed longer.

I've sketched a diagram of what that looks like – your speed decreases as you go further in your slide, and there's a narrow range of speeds that are right for the shot, where you should be releasing. If you slow down less fast by becoming more slippery, you stay in that zone longer (though you then have to launch out of the hack with closer to the right weight).

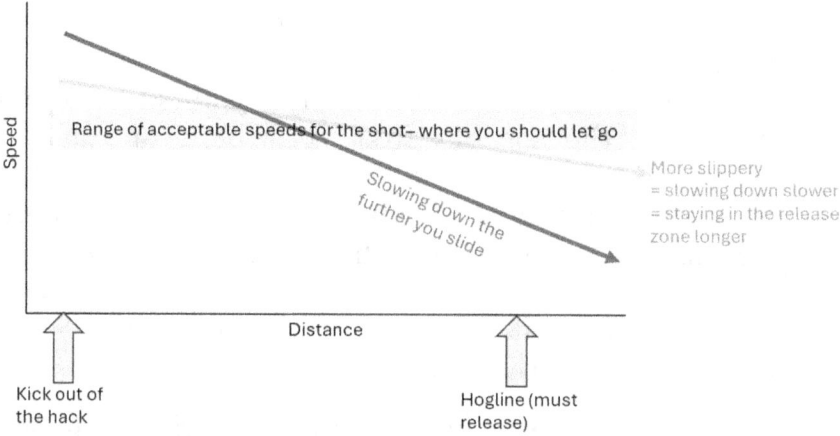

If you're decelerating slower (that is, more slippery), you'll have more time in your slide where you're in the right speed zone for making a shot, though the trade-off is that you'll have to be more precise in your kick to start (compare the less-steep light grey line to the steeper dark blue line in the totally number-less and arbitrary sketch above). It also means you don't have to kick as hard in the first place to over-come all that drag.

This is in part why moving up to dedicated curling shoes can be a good move if you're going to stick with the sport.

They should last a number of years (I kept my first pair of curling shoes for 16 seasons, which in hindsight was like 8 too many, but I was a student and the point is not to shame me for my frugality but to illustrate that you will get multiple years of use out of a pair so the per-season cost is not bad). They make you more slippery: the slider is more slippery, the trailing shoe won't have that slip-on gripper coming up around the toe to grab the ice, and you may even get a toe dip to make the trailing foot have even less drag.

Why We Don't Push

I'll say it explicitly: try not to push the rock to make a shot. There are three things we need to get right to make a shot: the direction (line), speed (weight), and rotation (handle). Each of those is pretty finicky and requires finesse and precision in curling. So by doing our crazy lunge slide, we can try to give ourselves time to finely apply each, and more importantly, to separate out each of the components.

The rotation you put on at the end with the "handshake release".

The direction you set by lining up carefully in the hack and sliding to the broom.

And the weight [*insert answer here once I figure it out myself*]. I mean, you kick out and slide and then decelerate until you get in the window, which requires some feel and experience.

And you do all of those with different body parts: you line your hips and shoulders up square to the broom to hit the line. You drive with your legs then slide on your foot to get to the right weight. You use your wrist and fingers to add the rotation.

If you push/shove the rock, suddenly you have to get all three right in unison, with one movement, with one body part (your arm), in a split second. It's rarely successful, and a bad habit – I know when I'm skipping, I'd rather you slide nice to the broom and hog the rock than realize you're too light and give the rock a crazy shove where you may not make the shot anyway and I won't learn anything about that line. One may get the outcome for that rock right, but not help you make the next shot (or next hundred shots) in your curling career any better. If you work with sweepers who time your delivery, pushing the rock makes it impossible for them to use the stopwatch as an aid for their sweeping calls.

For those with the bad habit of shoving the rock, the big question I think about is if you are going to shove the rock... *why slide first*? Then you're shoving from an unstable, slippery place while you are yourself moving. If (again, don't, but hypothetically) you're going to just shove the rock, you're probably better off doing it from the hack where you're at least stable and can shove from a place of strength.

SLIDING AND BALANCE

So, so much in curling comes down to **balance**. You're trying to slide on a piece of slippery material on top of a slippery surface, with very few other points of contact (and very limited weight on those). If you don't get that slider foot *right* under your centre of gravity, you *will* fall.

If you're not well balanced on your slider, there are only so many other places your weight can go. There's your back foot. Your broom or stabilizer. And that's it.

Oh, **the rock**. The rock is there too... but only for *part* of the slide. If you start off leaning on the rock for support, you will have to shift your weight as you release, which *will* screw up your shot. Shifting your weight off of the rock to let it go will change the line, speed, or both.

Balance is fundamental to the traditional curling delivery: if you don't have good balance all kinds of other weird compensatory quirks can seep in, and it can be hard to correct without going back to balance.

Balancing in the Sliding Position

The first exercise to build up toward a full delivery is to get into that final slide position and get comfortable balancing on a very slippery piece of Teflon in a weird lunge position. You can do it first on dry land (without the slipperiness), which helps with stretching too.

Then on ice near the backboards where you can hold on to something firm and unmoving, slowly get down on top of that sliding foot (typically your non-dominant foot, so left foot for righties) and extend your other leg behind you, flipping the foot over so the sole is pointing up. Your slider foot is going to have to be fully underneath you, centred under your sternum or you will be very unsteady. Once you find the balance in the slide position, you can push yourself back and forth a little. Feel the ice slide under that slippery slider, feel the dynamic balance. Let go (briefly at first) of the backboard.

Own this position – you will be in it a lot for the sport of curling.

Broom and Stabilizers

For good stability and balance on ice, three points of contact are best. So in the sliding position with your slider foot centred under you, and your trailing leg spread far behind you, you have very good front-to-back stability: you are extremely unlikely to fall forward and smash your face, or flip around backward from that position. However, you're probably quite likely to tip over to one side or the other: your lateral stability on just your slider foot and the top side of the toes of your trailing leg is not going to be great.

This is where the broom or stabilizer* will come into play: they provide the lateral stability in your slide.

A broom is the traditional choice and has a big benefit of simplifying the equipment that you need. It can be a little trickier to learn, in part because it's hard to put much weight on the broom – you're forced to get most of your weight balanced on your slider foot. The flip side is that some curlers and teachers like focusing on the broom because it forces the curler to get their balance on their feet and not over-rely on the delivery aid.

When using a broom for stability, you'll want to have a little bit of "positive pressure", pushing it into the ice enough that it isn't going to wobble, and ensuring that if you are going to tilt off of your perfect balance over your slider foot, it will be in the direction of the broom to help hold you up. But not so much that you're leaning on it.

Generally, you'll want your shoulders to be square in the delivery (which helps with getting the line of delivery right), which means you'll need to hold your broom at about the height the other hand is on the rock. That'll be roughly a third of the way up the broom for most people, with the exact amount depending on the angle you hold the broom at.

The broom will then tend to wobble around if you're just holding it down near one end and pressing it gently into the ice, so you'll need a second point of contact for it

---

* There are a few nicknames for these devices: delivery aid, crutch, stabilizer... I will mostly use stabilizer.

further up the handle. That will be somewhere on your back, anywhere from your waistline up to your armpit. Some people prefer tucking it into the armpit for more stability, others find the broom goes into a better position to keep your shoulders square to the target (i.e., with the broom head out parallel to the rock) if the other end sits closer to your hip. I suggest trying to keep the head one the ice even with the rock and the handle end closer to your hip, but you'll find a position that works best for you with some practice.

Stabilizers are a little newer in the sport[*] but can generally be found in every club. In our Little Rock program we start all the kids with stabilizers. They provide a broader base on the ice than just the sliver of contact a broom provides, and a defined handle (ideally at the same height as the rock handle), so there isn't confusion about where to make another point of contact on your back.

It can be a little easier to find your balance and get up and running as a curler with a stabilizer, in part because it's a lot easier to put more of your weight on one, spreading out how you're balancing, and giving you another, more stable point forward of your slider foot to lean on when you have to let go of the rock. The danger is that you might over-rely on the stabilizer to keep you upright even with relatively poor balance on your slider foot – the rock may be getting way off line, you may have weight transfers off the rock, etc., that aren't as noticeable as when you start to get into those kinds of bad habits with a broom.

The other major downside to a stabilizer is that it's another piece of equipment to lug around. Not only do you have to bring it to the rink (and it may not fit in a narrow

---

[*] Morris' patent application is from 1996.

locker), you have to remember to bring it to the other end each time you switch ends*. That can sometimes slow down play when someone inevitably forgets their stabilizer and has to go trotting up and down the ice to retrieve it.

However, which to play with is ultimately up to you. If you throw better with a stabilizer, by all means use one. If you're able to deliver with a broom and prefer the simplicity in your life, go with that.

What Happens if You Don't Have Good Balance?

In a normal walk on dry land, our feet stay a little off-centre and move forward and behind our centre-of-mass, and everything is fine: friction helps hold our feet in place. But once you move to ice, with a slider on your foot, friction is a capricious ancient god that has forsaken you and your kin. If you are not balanced directly, completely, perfectly on top of your slider foot, the force will keep pushing your foot out in the direction it's already off-centre, and you will find your foot is no longer there to support you.

Unless you have another point of contact to help balance out your forces, which may be a broom or stabilizer… or the rock. The rock unconsciously but very commonly becomes one of those extra points to help you fix your balance issues. The major problem with that very natural, automatic solution is that *eventually you have to let go of the rock*. And if you're leaning down on it and have to shift your weight off of it to let go, that weight shift is going to change the trajectory of the rock – all your careful work to get the right weight and line is going to

---

* That or you buy *two*, which is a bit more of an outlay and stuff to lug to the rink.

be thrown off at the last second as you try not to fall on it when you let go.

How to Improve Your Balance

The best balance exercises involve not having a rock at all, because at some point in your delivery you won't have one.

If you're on the ice, there are a few ways to help figure out and practice your balance.

1. You can slide without a rock. You don't even have to do a full imagined delivery: just slide out without the pull-back and park phase. You don't need to go far, the point at this stage is balancing on that slider foot. This is also a good test of your balance: if you can slide out without a rock, you're likely ready to work on the other parts of your delivery.
2. You can go up to the backboards and get into the delivery position on your slider. Then, just gently push yourself forward and backward off the board to get a little bit of movement going and see how well you can balance without other support. Can you take your hands fully off the backboard? Where does your foot have to be under your body for that balance?

Other exercises can include sliding with two rocks or with your broom flat on the ice in front of you with both hands on it – leaning forward will help you find that balance on the slider foot, as you won't be able to use a rock or stabilizer closer to your core to lean on.

But those exercises require ice and practice ice can be hard to come by.

Curling for Beginners and Improvers

On dry land, you can work on holding the curling position and slight variations on it: instead of being right down on the ground in your lunge position, try standing with your sliding leg nearly straight and planted below you, your back leg back (parallel to the ground) and arms spread like a plane. Then lower down to the sliding position, and feel where your body moves to keep your weight centred over your foot as your knee bends and you get lower.

If you're standing with your leg straight, your balance point will probably be with your foot under or just slightly ahead of your hips (top panel for someone with dancer's

40

grace doing it, middle panel for me, an average curler practicing). As you lower yourself down, you'll feel the strength you need in your legs to hold that position (and what makes it a good off-ice workout), and also find that your body shifts back so that your foot ends up closer to being under your sternum, as it would be in the slide.

Setup in the Hack

Most hacks used by curling clubs are the kind with two sloped rubber bases, with a patch of ice between them. You may **not** pick and choose which hack to throw from depending on the shot – lefties throw from the right side, righties throw from the left side, always. Some clubs are transitioning to a single hack right on the centreline, but I expect it will be another generation before that really catches on.

Before getting into the hack, decide if you need to clean the bottom of the rock. In many cases, you'll be able to line up better if you get in the hack (for stability), clean the bottom of the rock, then stand up and reset. However, if you don't have the strength or coordination to flip the rock for cleaning without risking a smash in the ice (which the icemaker will not be happy about), the traditional split hack is wonderful for a life hack*: pull the rock back and upside-down on the hack to then clean the bottom. It helps hold it in place while cleaning and for the flip.

Approach the hack from the rear (this will be important in the section to come covering *Line of Delivery*), and get your hack foot (typically your dominant leg – left foot for lefties, right foot for righties) planted in the hack. Especially if you're using a step-on slider, get stable in the hack before stepping on to the slider.

You will want your foot up on the sloped part, with the ball of your foot near the centre of that sloped part. Unless you have particularly large feet, no part of your foot will be touching the flat part at the bottom of the hack. This is in part to give you more leverage and traction when pushing forward, and in part to provide a bit of space for your trailing foot to flip over as you get into the slide. The rock will be in front of your hack foot (more on that in *Line of Delivery*).

DELIVERY CADENCE

The next phase in the delivery after you get your balance is going through the motions of the slide. There's a lot happening in this action, so we break it down into discrete steps in the traditional delivery instructions:

1. Press forward
2. Hips up
3. Rock back, foot back
4. Pause
5. Rock forward, foot forward

---

* You bet that pun was fully intended and I am sitting here with my dad-joke grin on waiting for you to acknowledge it.

6. Slide

Each little motion happens in sequence, we sometimes call this sequence the *cadence*.

There's a very good reason for each of these components and for the order that we put them in. A good exercise is to practice this in super-slow-motion to be sure you're not getting a rogue body part moving ahead of its turn.

In that way it's kind of like learning a dance: you bring in the steps, very slowly, then slowly pick up the tempo until you're at full performance speed.

The basic gist of it is that by the time we're out and sliding we want that slider foot centred under us for good balance. But we don't *start* with our slider foot out front under our centre of mass – when we're in the hack it starts beside us, with our weight somewhere between 50-50 to mostly on that nice,stable hack foot.

(In the photo the rock is off to the side so you can see my feet – in a proper setup the rock would be on the line of delivery in front of my hack foot.)

[Forgive me using myself as a model – it's less than ideal for several reasons not least of which is that I'm throwing left-handed so most of you have to mirror this in your minds].

Before we can slide, we need that sliding foot to come around to the centre (centre of our bodies, on the line of delivery, not the centreline between the two hacks!). But we can't do that because the rock is there! There's a lot that has to happen to get moving down the ice along that line of delivery with good balance, and we do it in sequence.

First up: **press forward**. This is mostly to help unlock everything (as is the next part, hips up), but that press is also on the line of delivery and helps remind you that you'll be going in that direction. If something is misaligned to that line, the press is often a point where you may say hey, something's wrong, I'm going to stand up and reset. The press also helps ensure the rock didn't freeze in place while you were waiting in the hack for the call from your Skip or for a sweeper to get ready. That little forward motion will help make sure everything is moving and you won't get thrown off by some frost in a later step when you're already committed to the slide.

Then, **hips up**. It doesn't have to be much, we're not doing a yoga pose and trying to get our butts in the sky, but we have to unlock our ability to move the rest, which you can't do fully squatted in the hack.

Then **rock back** (rock goes first, always!), and just a split second after, **foot back**. The foot doesn't have to go back far – just far enough for the slider foot's toe to line up with the hack foot's heel (called the "heel-to-toe" position for short) is the conventional suggestion. Basically just enough to let you transfer your weight back a bit to get ready. That weight transfer also helps prepare the power to transfer back forward to get things moving.

And **pause**. When you deliver normally there's just a brief moment where you're not moving at all as you switch from pulling back to moving forward. But when practicing this in super-slow motion, you can really exaggerate that pause. The point is that you don't want to have conflicting motions, where your hips are still moving back while your shoulders are trying to get the rock forward. Pause and switch fully to forward gear.

In the pause, our hips are back behind the plane of the hack, and we have transferred some of our weight onto the sliding foot (50-50 weight distribution would be the high end – the hack is still the stable point to stand on), which is back in that heel-to-toe position.

Then **rock forward,** followed shortly thereafter by **foot forward**. That's because you need the rock to move forward to create space for your slider foot to come forward and in. You need that foot to come forward and in so you can balance on it before you start to engage the kick to actually slide. If your hack foot is kicking to drive you out into the delivery while your slider foot is still off-centre, it's going to be hard to maintain that nice balance.

We're shifting our weight forward to the hack foot, bringing the slider foot forward, and shifting the weight forward again to the slider foot.

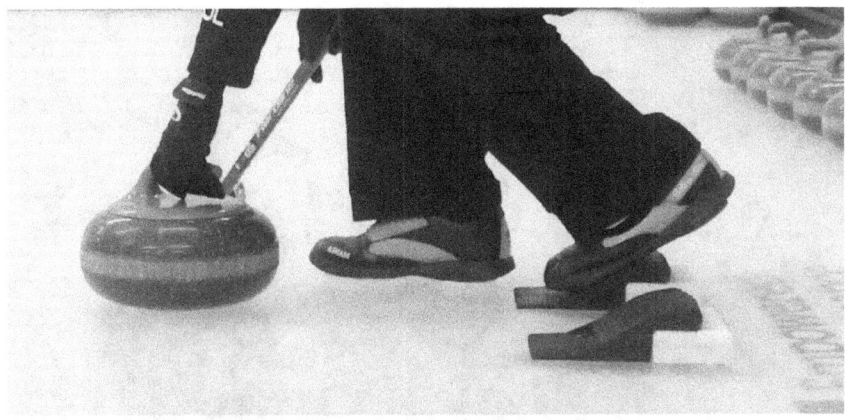

In this photo, my hips are still mostly elevated – I haven't kicked hard yet – and the rock is forward, my foot is just about in line, and now I could be balanced if I kicked. If I started my kick a few frames earlier, my foot would still be off to the side and I'd have to try to catch my balance while bringing it across. My eyes are also up at the target.

Finally, **slide**.

Even without a big kick from your hack leg, you'll generate some forward momentum from dropping your hips (going through the cadence faster and dropping them faster will help generate more weight), but this is generally where you will start to use those big leg muscles to propel you (and more importantly, the rock) forward to make your shot.

But it's like a dance. Even as you up the tempo, you have to keep the order of the steps the same. You still need that slider foot under you and in a position to take your weight before you can engage those powerful leg muscles to explode out of the hack. So practice slow, get the order of the steps, and then pick up the tempo. Press, hips, rock back, foot back, *pause**, rock forward, foot forward, slide.

Some delivery and balance issues can be caused by getting the timing wrong. Most often trying to slide before the foot is fully on your line and under you, or trying to get the foot forward and around in front before the rock has moved forward to make the space, forcing one or the other off the line. Rock, then foot, then slide.

The final form has the rock in front of your sliding foot, ideally all on one line pointed at the target (covered more in the next section). Perhaps under your nose, perhaps centred under your dominant eye, but somewhere in that range to help your hand-eye coordination keep the rock on that line. Note in the image above that is not quite the case, with the rock appearing a bit to the right side of the image (my left), which may be a mistake on my part in that throw, or a parallax error from perhaps not sliding right at the camera.

Your trailing leg will usually have the knee get *close* to the ice but, ideally, not touch it. Depending on your level of flexibility, you may be able to drop your body closer to the ice, or you may be a little more upright in posture, as I am in this photo:

---

* Emphasis added not because the pause has to be a long one, but because it's so often skipped entirely. In game it may just be a fraction of a second, but enough to re-synchronize all the moving parts for the switch to forward motion.

LINE OF DELIVERY

Lining up to the broom is so critical to make a shot. Moreover, lining up to the broom is a *technique thing*: you should be able to hit (or get pretty close) to the broom pretty much every time. (Weight is a *feeling* thing and changes all the time – you will hear multiple times through the book how much trouble I still have with it despite two decades of curling under my belt.)

As a Skip, from the far end of the ice, I can often spot when someone is going to miss the broom before they even start their slide: they just haven't lined up properly in the hack, or different body parts are pointing at different targets.

So the two main take-home messages for this chapter are:

1) You should line up to the broom as you get into the hack every time, and all body parts should line up to the same target.

2) Everything moves on that line of delivery.

The first step though is to actually *visualize* that line of delivery. Draw that imaginary line from your hack (not the empty space in-between the two hacks) to the Skip's broom (your target).

Then right from when you approach* the hack, *everything* is going to be lining up to that line. Your toes (both hack foot and then after that's planted, slider foot) are going to point to the Skip's broom. Your belly button will point there. Your shoulders and hips are square to that broom. The rock is brought to the line of delivery. Your nose and eyes are pointed to the broom.

Now as shorthand, guides will often talk about one of those many body parts so it's not such an exhaustive list: point your toe, or your knee, or your belly button, or square your shoulders. When I use one body part as a shorthand, I like to use the hips. Because as Shakira says: *hips don't lie.*

Your hips are a central attachment point: if your knee is pointed one way and your shoulders another, you're probably going to end up going where your hips point. And as a Skip that's also the easiest to spot clue that you're going to miss — if I'm standing way on one side of the house and your hips are pointing to the other side of centre (or off to the other sheet), I know you're going to miss my broom.

Anyway, so you're getting into the hack and everything (toes to nose and especially hips in-between) is pointed at that broom. Then you have to do all of your motions along

---

* I'll note that if you're doing a good job of playing quickly (getting your rock to the hack and cleaning it before the last team's rock has even finished moving), you will likely have to stand back up and wait for your skip to put the broom down. You can then line up as you get into the hack for the *second* time. If you stay squatting down from cleaning your rock, it can be hard to properly reset your position; likewise, stand up to reset if your skip moves the target on you.

that same line. Your press forward to loosen the rock at the beginning is *on that line.* Your pullback is *on that line.* Your push out and slide is – say it with me! – ON THAT LINE.

Sometimes I think the centreline painted on the sheet does us a disservice because I see many curlers want to stick to it, doing some movements (e.g., the forward press) along a line to centre, then trying to fix it during the kick or even after they're sliding to hit the broom. Similarly, many new curlers seem to have issues with brooms placed out on the wings – it's just a line to follow. It's no harder to draw one from your foot to the 12' than it is from your foot to the button. Plus they're not that different from each other: at the near hog line it's only about two feet of spread from one extreme part of the house to the other. Yet it still seems to be a common mental block.

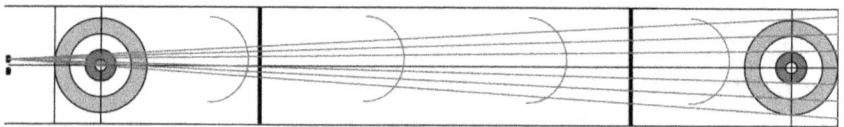

From the hack, the spread of lines to either edge of the far house is not very big – just a few feet of difference at the near hog line.

If you're taking that moment to line up to the broom as you enter the hack, making sure all of your movements then continue to stay on that line connecting your starting point in the hack with the target at the other end, then you should hit the line pretty much every time. Once you do that, you can start making a lot of shots. Indeed, the sport changed forever[*] when some teams discovered that they could have nearly 100% success throwing hits because weight was a matter of finesse but line was easy to get consistent with the right technique.

There is a little bit of fuzziness on what *exactly* it means to bring the rock to the line of delivery. That is generally going to be somewhere in front of your hack foot (and not

---

[*] See the 2019 Netflix series *Losers,* episode 4.

on the centreline or between the two halves of the hack). But whether that's going to be under your armpit, under your nose, or under your dominant eye is a bit of a point of disagreement amongst coaches and players.

I say as long as it's "on the line" where *you* expect it to be for *your* hand-eye coordination, and you do that consistently, then it's going to work for you. Your hand-eye coordination may expect it to be right under your dominant eye, or maybe a touch off to the side, near the armpit (i.e., the shoulder that is pushing it).

GRIP AND RELEASE

Eventually we do have to let go of the stone. We want to be able to impart that nice rotation about the rock's centre without screwing up the line and weight that we spent so much time establishing with our body alignment and our slide.

When holding the stone, you want to have your fingers curled underneath the handle, nice and even, with your index finger up close to the front. Your thumb comes down around the side. Your wrist stays high.

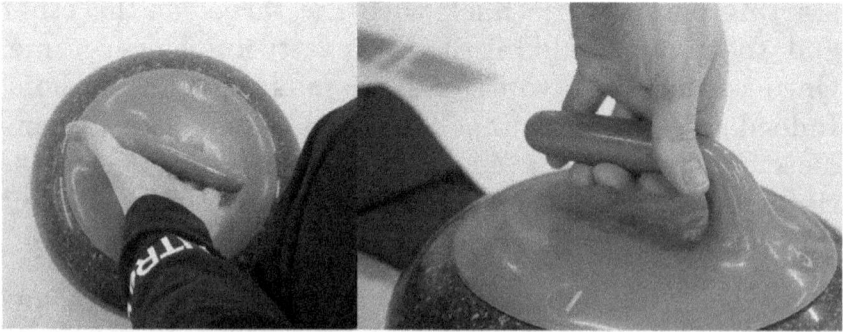

You start with the handle at the 10 o'clock or 2 o'clock position, depending on the call from your Skip. Then you hold it there through the slide. In the last few feet before your release point, simply give it a turn back toward 12 o'clock and open your hand.

It sounds easy in text. It looks pretty easy in this photo:

I like to discuss **why** we do it this way.

For the grip, we talk about keeping the wrist high with just the fingers on the rock because we don't want you leaning on it – think back to the first component, balance: we don't lean on the rock because we're planning to let go of it real soon. It's not a great long-term solution to the problem of not falling on your face on slippery ice. If you're letting your wrist droop and getting the palm on there, it's easier to just lean on it, maybe without even noticing until you have to make that weight shift.

Imagine spikes coming out of the top of the handle to prevent you from leaning on it.

We also want the fingers up front because then you can rotate the rock around its centre: all you want to do here is rotate the rock around its axis, not push it off the line.

This is where that starting at 10 and 2 thing comes into play: there's so much to think about when throwing the stone during the delivery that you don't also want to think about which handle to put on at the last minute. So if you turn the stone while you're in the hack to the appropriate side while you have a second to think, you then just have to turn it back to centre at release. It becomes automatic. And consistent if you do it at the same point in your delivery each time.

And as always, there are exceptions: Shannon Birchard (4-time [so far] Canadian women's champion) infamously starts with a dirty, dirty counter-rotation and then snap back. It clearly works for her. But *generally* keeping things simpler and cleaner is going to help you be more consistent.

So in the last two to three feet of your slide, as you feel you're in the window for weight (which is hopefully at the same point of your slide most of the time but sometimes may be a little further or closer to the near hog line), you start your rotation from the initial position of 10 or 2 back to 12 o'clock.

As for how many rotations, for years the advice was to aim for 2-3 rotations as the stone moved down the ice, but lately the recommendation is to aim for 3-4 (and even more on tournament ice). The smaller the distance in the last part of your slide that you do your turn back to centre, the more final rotations you'll end up with (i.e., the faster the rock will be spinning). That basically means that the newer rule of thumb is to put your turn on over the last 2-3 feet of your slide, while the older advice was to do it over 3-4 feet. Really as long as you're consistent, anything in there will work for club play. If you join a more competitive team, you'll likely all work to agree on a single value to get your releases to match better.

And finally, that "handshake" release, letting go as our wrists bring the hand back around to the 12 o'clock position: that's so that we don't over-rotate the stone and "get it started", that is, start sending it off the line of delivery. If you start at 10 and end at 2 (or vice-versa), you'll likely see that you'll have stones that get off the line or seem to "curl right out of your hand" more often than someone with a neutral release at 12 o'clock.

Let's compare and contrast all of this with another common grip that you'll see the pros use, particularly those with a tuck delivery: holding it from the back of the handle, wrist behind the rock. If you want to search for some video clips, Kevin Koe's got a grip like this, as do many European players.

I know he makes a lot of really touch shots and nails the line with massive weight. I have no earthly idea *how* he does it without accidentally setting the stone off its course – holding back there seems like you'd naturally lever the rock off the line as you try to rotate it. So obviously there are other ways to make all of this work and get the stone to where you want it... but there's a reason the traditional Curling Canada approach is to teach high-wrist hand centred over the rock rather than holding it just by the tip.

DELIVERING WITH A STICK

All of the previous advice about how to manage the traditional delivery assumes that you can get down into the hack and then slide in some approximation of all of that. For some of us, whether due to a lack of balance, permanent mobility issues, or temporary injuries, that just isn't possible.

Curling is an inclusive sport, and we want a place for those who struggle with the traditional delivery to be able to play, too, and thankfully we have the delivery stick for them to use.

I would love to say with complete honesty that there is no shame in using a delivery stick, but I know many people don't want to "feel old" for using one, as it is more common in older players. I, for one, will think no less of you for choosing one (indeed, I will cheer you on because it means you get to participate in this wonderful, quirky sport with me and aren't missing out). I can say that several of the top 20 spots in our club are occupied by stick curlers: they are every bit as able to make precise draws and hits as those of us who get down and slide.

Instead I will implore you to put that pride aside and if a stick is the right call for you, just grab one and don't hurt yourself down on the ice. Become a weapon with it. Most importantly, have fun and participate with it – it's a tool to help you.

The general idea is that you will use two grippers on your feet (though there are a few stick curlers who slide standing up with it), use the stick to bring the rock with you while you move upright, walk up to speed toward the Skip's broom/target, and then rotate the rock as you release.

The principles of delivering with a stick are the same as for a slide delivery: you want to deliver a stone with a precise weight, line, and rotation.

You want to separate out those components in time and muscle groups for maximum precision.

So, setup in the hack will start with getting your line of delivery right. As with the slide delivery, you'll start with the rock in front of your hack foot, on the line of delivery (with some flexibility in what precisely that means to you). You'll generally want the stick on some predictable line, too, which to me means bringing it to my belly button, but may be skewed one side or the other for you. Line up your hips (and everything else) to the Skip's broom. Your stick position and rock position should support the notion that every part of you can start pushing out of the hack and walk straight toward your Skip's broom – if not, you may need to make some adjustments.

Just as with the sliding delivery, you'll set your rotation while still in the hack, releasing back to centre at the end. For many stick players, 10 and 2 is the *maximum* angle the stick will accommodate, and the handle is typically started at closer to 10:30-11 or 1-1:30 than true 10 and 2.

Then, you walk toward the target broom. Unlike the slide delivery, instead of *decelerating* through the slide, you are typically *accelerating* as you move forward, until you get to the correct speed for the shot (which, sadly, is again a feeling thing that I can't provide absolute guidance for). Then you apply a rotation – often over a shorter distance though starting from a less-rotated angle to achieve a similar 2–4 total rotations down the ice.

In some cases, you *may* need to push the stone with the stick to get the right speed. However, if you are able to walk fast enough (including for take-outs), it's a good idea to avoid that for the same reasons we don't push on the slide delivery: you don't want to set the rock off the line you worked so hard to stick to.

A follow-through is a very good idea. A common source of falls is people trying to stop dead from the fastest part of their stick delivery, and then over-compensating and falling backward. Use a few steps to decelerate slowly after releasing the rock. Another suggestion is to lean slightly forward when you release.

SHOT TOLERANCE

Curling can be a game of extreme precision. We see that on TV in the Scotties, Brier, and Slams, with some incredible draws and highly precise hits and run-backs.

Most of the time in recreational curling, we don't have to be that precise: we have **tolerance** in the shot. A little light may be good; sometimes heavy is fine. I try when I'm skipping to show what the tolerance is ("draw here is good, but leaving a guard works too" or "try to freeze but better to be heavy and tap it than come up light"), but a lot of the time it's implied.

Basically, a wide range of outcomes are still considered "made" shots. This is important to keep in mind, particularly as new curlers, because precision shots are so very difficult in this sport. Just because the Skip taps the broom in the house doesn't mean that a guard isn't also a "made" shot.

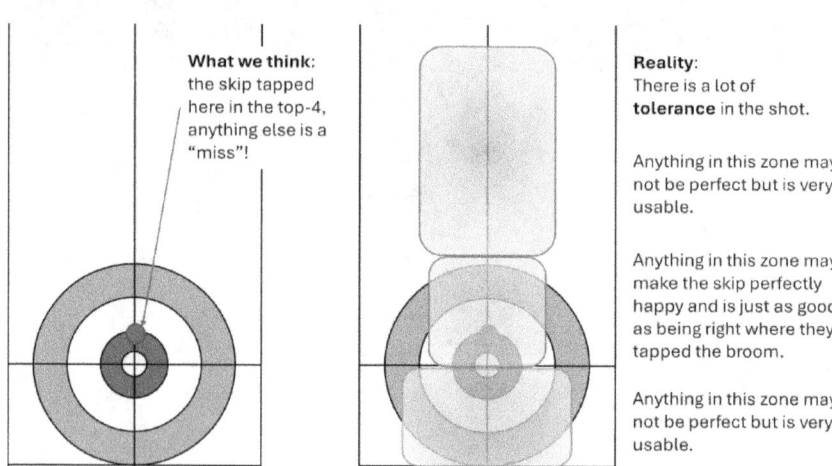

What we think: the skip tapped here in the top-4, anything else is a "miss"!

Reality: There is a lot of **tolerance** in the shot.

Anything in this zone may not be perfect but is very usable.

Anything in this zone may make the skip perfectly happy and is just as good as being right where they tapped the broom.

Anything in this zone may not be perfect but is very usable.

For the Skips (myself included), let's try to be good about explicitly showing the tolerance. Everyone likes to be successful in their hobbies. For the newer curlers it's important to know that sometimes a shot can be ten or more feet off of where the Skip tapped the ice and still be a made shot! That's just the nature of the game and nearly every time we raise our hand and yell "good shot" we really do mean it!

For those of you who are newer, the Skips (including me) aren't always going to remember to show the tolerance, so I'll try to give some general rules of thumb. Usually when playing a draw or guard (especially the first few rocks), the tolerance is usually to be light – stopping in the top 4' may be the perfect call, for example, but being 10' light and leaving a guard is still a successfully made shot.

Plus, **you have sweepers who can help a light rock travel a little further, but who can't do anything but stand and watch a heavy one.** Nonetheless, much of the time, a rock that's a *little bit* heavier is still fine and usable.

For hits, throwing straight to the broom is often the most important part, as there will typically be more room for tolerance on the speed than the line. Even if the shot is missed, by sliding and releasing straight to the broom, you will help your Skip adjust the call for the next attempt. Even if it clips a guard or sails past everything, it can give the Skip important information about what the ice is doing with hit weight, or open up a new path to make the next hit attempt easier – if you miss the target rock but also missed the Skip's broom then the Skip may just have to give the same shot attempt again and hope you hit the broom. In terms of outcomes, usually we'll show which way we'd prefer the shot stone to roll, but as long as you make contact with the stone to be hit, it's generally a successful shot. When coming up to freeze to the other team's rock, a little heavy may be the "pro miss" as you may not want to give them a guard... but there are situations where it may be the opposite.

Most of the time at the recreational level, our main goal (particularly with the first 10 rocks) is to get rocks in play, and there's lots of ways to make that happen.

THROWING A HIT

Through the previous sections on how to deliver a stone, I didn't talk much about weight control.

Getting the weight right is, in my opinion, the hardest part about curling. The ice changes all the time and weight is all about *feeling*. You can line up and hit the broom every time, but it's hard to deliver a stone at a given velocity each time. And even if you can get your technique down to push off just right for a given speed in an objective measure like m/s, that speed may not be the right one for draw weight on a given night (or even a given end in a single game) because of changing ice conditions.

But hey, you can get it pretty close. And the **tolerance** is often pretty wide – if you don't get it in the house, a guard will probably work too (especially early in the end).

Moreover, draws and guards are very forgiving for other errors. If you miss the broom (line of delivery), or do something funky on your release that affects the curl or the line, you're probably still going to get a draw/guard out of the shot, just in a different spot.

A hit attempt is much less forgiving on line and release errors: if you miss the line, or get it started on release, you'll likely miss the target rock and go sailing out of play.

However, if you *do* hit the line, it's fairly forgiving on weight. And because hits tend to run straighter, they can be more predictable.

If you watch the Netflix Series *Losers*, one of the episodes is on the Pat Ryan team that figured this magic out: while making good draws may be hard (really hard for some of us), if you're consistently hitting the broom for line, you can be pretty confident you can get a rock out of play. You may hit one side of the rock versus another if you're a little light or heavy, but as long as you hit the broom with something in the right range, the hit is made. And made pretty darned consistently.

So they started to play a game where they'd score 1, then hit everything. Blank end, blank end, blank end, game over, 1-0. It was in response to this discovery of the power of hitting that the free guard zone came into being, but now I'm going too far down the curling history rabbit hole.

That consistency comes because hitting the broom is not a fussy matter of feel that changes through the game and from rink to rink like draw weight – getting the line right is a *matter of technique*, and with some practice you can do it every time.

The main takeaway is that to get good at hits, you "just" have to get good at hitting the broom, that is, mastering your line of delivery.

Now, "just" is in those well-deserved air quotes because there are lots of things in life that are easy for some people and not others, lots of times where it's a useful short-hand to those with experience but a daunting proposition for someone new, and lots of things that are easy to say but hard to do ("just" lose 30 lbs my doctor says). But again, hitting the broom is a technique thing. So it can be done consistently fairly early in your curling career (whereas I've spent nearly 25 years on the ice and still *quite often* put my guards all the way through the house).

The other part of making a hit is getting the weight.

Defining Hit Weights

To take a rock out of play doesn't actually require that much extra force in your delivery. You will lose some energy in the collision, but a rock that would go past the backline by just 2–3' has enough energy to hit another rock and make it go out of play... as long as the hit is pretty solid*. Of course, you can also throw killer weight and get that rock and two of its closest friends moving out of the house, but that's not *necessary* to start making hits.

Generally, we talk about a handful of different hit weights, which also make it easier to communicate with your Skip on a noisy sheet. Each club or region of the world may have different names for roughly the same ideas (I hear "Easy" and "Firm" from several Canadian teams West of Thunder Bay that sounds like they mean what I would call "Control" and "Normal"). If you join a long-term team you'll likely settle on your own vernacular that may not be any of these terms. Nonetheless, as a starting point here are the names for the various hit weights I'm most familiar with.

Hack: The lightest true hit is called "**hack**" – just enough for the thrown rock to go through the house and stop at about the hack on the other end. That will let you hit a rock not quite on the nose and still get it out of play. Skips will often communicate hack weight by touching their heel or pointing at the hacks behind them with their broom.

Hack is really only a few feet heavier than a draw – about 6' more than the backline or 12' more than T-line weight – many of us throw hack by accident when attempting a

---

* "Solid" here means close to the centre of the rock, to transfer more momentum from the thrown stone to the target stone. Sometimes solid for hits means travelling faster.

draw*! So it doesn't take a great deal of strength or a change in your slide: often you can get to hack weight by using the same kick and slide and just releasing a few feet sooner in your slide.

In many cases, because hack is all you need to get a rock out of play, if you're not comfortable throwing more weight, you can ask a Skip calling for a hit to give you a hack weight hit – let them figure the ice out for what you're comfortable throwing.

The downside to hack weight is that it is still light enough that there will be a fair bit of curl, so it's a little more likely to miss entirely and a little more challenging for a Skip to pick the right spot for the broom.

Board: The next increment we usually talk about is **board** weight, which is something like 6–10' more than hack. A board weight stone would sail through the house, still have some energy to move past the hack, and hit the back bumper with enough left to give a small bounce. Skips will usually communicate board weight by tapping their hip, or sometimes the boards themselves.

Board is a little more predictable than hack – most nights at our club a board weight shot will curl something like 1-2 rock widths, so if you start with the broom about a rock width from the target stone, you've got a good chance of hitting it on one side or the other.

You do have to start generating more speed in your delivery (more on that in a bit) to get to board weight, but it's still a very reasonable throwing speed. Most people find they can still throw board with good balance and lots of control.

Control and the other up-weight shots: There are a few increments beyond that: **control**, "**normal**", **peel**, which

---

* It's not *just* me, but also, it is *especially* me.

are generally each a step up in speed, something like the step up from hack to board*. But it starts to get harder to generate those weights and still hit the broom consistently with a balanced slide, at least until you have a chance to practice it a bit.

For these, a common sign from the Skip is to tap somewhere on the arm: down at the wrist for control, near the elbow for normal, up on the shoulder for peel (I even have a sweater with those printed on the arms, which you'll see me wear in many of the photos for this book). But teams will have their own jargon and way of communicating for these higher weight shots – some may instead call for "firm" rather than "normal", while other teams specify their hit weights in terms of the time it takes to go hog line to hog line (so a 9-second hit is faster than a 10-second hit).

Anyway, whatever you call it, "control" would be more than board, but still where many (but not all now!) curlers would find they can still have a nice, controlled, balanced slide and release. With control, you can roll a fair bit after a hit or get two rocks out of play if the double is reasonably well lined-up, or get a fairly straight, predictable trajectory even if the ice is fairly swingy. If you're using hog-to-hog times on rocks, control is something like a second (maybe 1.5 seconds depending on how your team defines it) faster than board. "Normal" is faster yet, enough that you can pick a rock out of play even just hitting an inch or two on the outside, or make a double even if you're hitting the first on a bit of an angle. If you don't hit your target fairly thick, there's a good chance you'll lose the shot rock throwing a normal weight takeout. For normal, you'll often start to put the broom

---

* If you're using hog-to-hog times, a rough rule of thumb is that each increment in named hit times is *about* a second faster (shorter). Board may be 11 seconds hog-to-hog, Control 10, Normal 9, Peel 8.

right on the target rock as it will only curl half a rock or less on most nights. And finally, peel is the maximum speed many people can throw. It's fast enough that even hitting a little off nose will see the shooter roll away, and can get a lot of granite moving. And I jammed them all into one paragraph because you probably won't see a lot of calls for those higher weight shots until you get into more competitive leagues.

Hitting Which Spot

As you get better at hits, you may start calling for a shot to hit a specific part of a rock, in which case it's helpful to have some common language around the parts of a rock.

If you imagine a perfectly direct hit from one circular rock to another, we would call that "on the nose". A *solid* or *thick* hit would be one that is closer to being on the nose, a *thin* hit is one that is further from being on the nose.

You can use those terms on their own: "hit it pretty thick," or you can use them to modify another description "I want to get a thick quarter."

For something a little more precise, a common approach is to describe how much overlap the two rocks (shooter and target) would have in the collision, expressed as a fraction of a rock. Nose or dead on would be a full overlap. "Half a stone" would be when the edge of the shooter is overlapping with the nose of the target, so there is half a rock of overlap between them. A "quarter rock" would be even less overlap, "seven eighths" would be nearly on the nose.

You can also use distances from the nose or from the edge. For small distances from the nose, it doesn't matter whether you're talking distances laterally or along the circumference of the rock*, for larger ones (or starting from the edge) you'll probably use the overlap method above or just point at the spot rather than get fussy about measurement conventions.

Generating Hit Weight

To get your weight up for hits, there are a few tricks.

The first and more obvious is to kick harder with your hack foot as you explode into the slide.

The next is to go through your cadence (press forward – rock back – foot back – pause – *rock forward – foot forward – slide*) **faster**. Dropping your hips in that slide part helps transfer some potential energy from gravity into kinetic energy moving forward.

If you don't already have the ball of your foot up on the sloped part of the hack, you can move your foot up to get a little more leverage for the kick. You can also accentuate the weight transfer in the pause portion – be sure you're getting those hips behind the plane of the hack, put some weight on the slider foot as it rests behind your hack foot. Then transfer the weight back to hack foot then slider foot.

And finally, you can start your release earlier in the slide. Remember, after you've left the hack all you're doing is slowing down. So releasing sooner can help get the weight up, particularly when moving from a heavy draw to hack weight.

It can be a little tricky to get the hang of throwing more power into your slide to get a hit. As you work toward that, you have to be careful not to introduce weird elements to try to get the speed up that will compromise

---

* I will not bring up middle school geometry for those who would rather leave it behind.

the rest of your delivery (especially ones that send you off line). A common one is to try to kick faster, but if you kick before you get your slider foot into position it can throw you off balance. Another common one is to try to swing your slider foot around to *throw* it forward to get some momentum, which can generate off-line movement (e.g., swinging your slider foot so hard it goes past your centreline and you fall trying to slide on it, or kicking your slider foot way, way behind you in the pullback then trying to fling it forward, twisting your hips off the line of delivery in the process).

For stick curlers, generating more weight will come partly from getting up to speed faster (i.e., walking/jogging faster before release) and partly from an arm extension adding some additional speed at release. As with the slide delivery, you'll want to try to separate out the components of the delivery as much as possible: if you can walk/jog up to hack or board weight speeds and use those for your hits, then you won't have to worry about an extra arm extension putting the rock off-line during release. However, for some people with mobility issues it may be an unavoidable compromise to use the arm in addition to the feet to generate hit weight.

As you work up to being able to generate different hit weights while still hitting the broom, bear in mind that the same signals the Skip uses for communicating weight can be used from the thrower back to the Skip. If you're only comfortable throwing hack weight and your Skip is trying to call control for you, go ahead and stand up and tap your foot: "How about with hack?"

Your Unique Delivery

The previous sections introduced the "Curling Canada" style delivery: flat foot, no lift, slide out. That's not the only way to deliver a stone, which may have been hinted at by the fact that modifying adjectives are needed at all.

There's a lot of logic behind each of the parts of the Curling Canada delivery and a reason we teach it that way. It's pretty well field-tested to get people up and running quickly and successfully making shots.

But at the end of the day, you don't have to have a perfect Curling Canada style delivery. Lots of pros are very successful with various idiosyncrasies, not to mention the fact that many people learn things like the Manitoba Tuck which look quite a bit different but still work.

Whatever delivery you've settled on may work for you, or maybe it could do with some tweaks (maybe back towards that idealized delivery, maybe not). It can be tough to say: is it working for you, tailored to your body's ability and personal style, or have you picked up some bad habits that just aren't serving you? Let's go through a few examples in different parts of the delivery and discuss a bit.

No Lift

"No lift" is to distinguish from an older style of delivery where players would lift and swing the rock back. Indeed, this style of delivery is what gives us the quirky split hack: that space in the middle was needed for the rock to come through in the backswing (some clubs are now shifting to a single hack on the centreline for both righties and lefties to use).

A core part of the modern delivery (for tuck curlers too) is to keep the rock flat on the ice. I'm old enough (or perhaps to put it more favourably, started curling young enough) that in my first year of Little Rocks, they were still teaching us to swing the rock back and up along the centreline – though the year after they reversed course and tried to switch us all to no-lift deliveries.

For a while we had a weird hybrid delivery, where we kept the rock on the ice, but also brought it back in-between the two hacks as part of our pull-back (and maybe tilted it back without entirely turning it into a pendulum). It wasn't until years later that I had someone correct me to pull it back on a line closer to the line of delivery (with various pointers of to my throwing arm shoulder or to my hack foot toe or whatever, but the main point is that it didn't have to be anywhere near the centreline).

If you are lifting your rock, it's likely that you learned 30 years ago and haven't unlearned it. If it's working for you, fine, but if you're newer to the sport and are doing it just because that's what you saw on TV ages ago (or some pros more recently), you should probably stop. This is one of the idiosyncrasies that's a little more cut and dry and so easier to address: there's almost no good reason to do it, and lots of good reasons to stop. You should probably unlearn any form of lift in your delivery. Really the only exception would be if you've been curling for a few decades and that's just the way you throw (in which case you're probably not listening to me anyway).

The backswing delivery requires more overall movement, so more complexity and more possibilities for something to go wrong. For example, a chance of dropping the rock if it slips out of your grasp, the likelihood of chipping the ice near the hacks where it makes contact again, and of course, starting the rock off of the line of delivery (or at least, having your body and the rock on different lines). It's hard to do just one part of a backswing delivery for practice or to correct a delivery error.

Flat Foot

Calling the delivery "flat foot" is to distinguish it from a "tuck" style delivery where the thrower is sliding up on their toes/front of their foot.

At a development session I was at, Ian Tetley told the story of starting off by sliding on his toe and in the 90's Wayne Middaugh telling him to unlearn that if he wanted to have a long career in this sport. There are good reasons to keep your slider foot flat on the ice: you get more stability, and it's easier on the joints.

I haven't had much luck finding stats on whether tuck-sliders *do* end up with more knee injuries in their careers. I haven't even spent enough time watching the senior championships to see if the proportion of tuck sliders decreases vs. the Brier and Scotties for some anecdotal evidence. But the received wisdom is that getting up on your toe is putting more strain on your knee and is a bad idea. While I'd love to take more evidence-based-medicine type approach here, sometimes it's not feasible to do without disappearing into a PubMed rabbit hole, so received wisdom will have to suffice*.

But being up on your toe *does* mean you shrink your contact surface with the ice, which can help you slide that tiny bit faster. More importantly, it can also help you lean forward and get your head a little closer to the ice, by letting your ankle provide some of the flexibility that your hip may lack (but again, at the expense of strain on your

---

* My editors said I should go ahead and drop down the research rabbit hole. However, I simply can't find hard stats to prove that tuck sliders do indeed sustain long-term injuries at a greater rate than flat foot sliders. The best I can find in terms of evidence against the tuck slide is a paper by Iona Robertson et al. (no relation), BMJ Open Sport Exerc Med. 2017; 3(1): e000221, that looked at the forces involved and confirmed that toe sliding does put much higher stress on the knee joint than flat-foot sliding.

knee). If you're a tucker and finding success with it, good for you! Though *you* should perhaps do the research to make sure that you're not increasing your risk of injury and joint wear with that slide.

If you are not doing a full tuck, but merely getting your heel just a bit off of the ice with your body in an otherwise "standard" delivery position, then it's really not likely to be serving you – you're adding that strain on your knee and decreasing your stability for really no benefit. Remember: *flat foot* delivery!

Slider Foot Movement

The way people move their slider foot in the delivery is an area where we'll start to see a lot of different successful variations on the standard delivery. When moving from resting next to the hack to being fully in the slide, there are lots of paths that slider foot can follow.

The standard method is straight forward a bit, straight back with a weight transfer – to just the heel-to-toe position – to moving forward and then in front to be centred under the body in the sliding position.

But you'll see some people not even bring their slider behind the hack foot, they just go forward from their set-up. Without the weight transfer, they should in theory not be able to kick quite as hard. However, that's fine: especially with fast sliders and a toe dip (see the *Equipment* section), it doesn't take much leg drive at all to generate enough power for a draw or even a down-weight hit. Indeed, I often struggle to not accidentally throw my draws right through the house and may actually benefit from not having the weight transfer for those shots. So again, find what works for your unique delivery.

And there are those on the other side of the spectrum, who bring the sliding foot much further back in the pull-back. Some people will lift their slider foot up and *step* into the position for sliding, rather than sliding it around (particularly for hits). Some will have a crescent movement to the whole process rather than a mostly straight forward/straight back motion until the final part of getting under the centre of the body.

Some of these can be the sources of errors, and some can just be your own unique style, or adapting to the way your hips want to allow you to move. If you're not making shots (getting off line, having poor balance), it can be good to go back to the standard delivery to make sure that your unique foot movement isn't throwing something off. But if you're balanced and hitting the line and happy with whatever you're doing, then have fun.

In particular, watch for bringing the sliding foot too far back: the power mostly comes from shifting your hips and weight back to the slider foot, then back to the hack foot, then forward again to the slider foot. The slider foot only has to go *just* behind the hack foot to accomplish that – any further back is more likely just putting your hips off-line or making it *harder* to transfer weight to the slider foot, as well as forcing you to move it faster to get it all the way back to the front to be in position to slide on.

The step forward is very common when throwing up-weight hits, and I'm fine with it. The crescent motion, however, should be watched. If it's working for you and that's your unique delivery, fine… but it's often an error that can cause wobbles as you try to get the slider foot under you in the beginning of the slide.

Slider Foot Orientation

Moving your slider foot a little toe-out, so the arch of your foot starts to come to face forward a little more can help a bit with lateral stability in the slide. Personally, my sliding knee's MCL screams *"no no no no no"* as soon as I get more than about 10° off of having my toe pointed to the broom, so I slide with a pretty straight foot. You'll find your own position that balances your knee's happiness with your stability, whether that's with your toes pointed right at the broom or 45° out to the side.

Trailing Leg

If you look at my left shoe (as a leftie, my hack foot), you'll see the massive wear pattern in the lace cover because I am someone who drags my whole damned foot behind me. Lots of pros are just on the tops or tips of their toes for the trailing foot. Some people will have a bend in their knee, others will have it straighter. Some may find they have to put a little turn in their ankle one way or the other.

Again, lots of little variations that may not affect your delivery much, though if you notice that your trailing leg is causing drag (and especially if it's causing a fish-tail that throws you off line), you may want to try to modify your positioning. Alternatively, you can modify your shoes (e.g., with a toe cover to reduce friction or a pair with a lace cover if the whole top of your foot makes contact like mine).

Sometimes, people may have much larger changes in what they do with their trailing leg. For instance, you may have a different kind of "tuck" delivery which is somewhat common: people who can't (or don't want to) fully extend their trailing leg, and tuck it back in to their body, sometimes even sitting on the trailing knee. I have seen this called a "meatball" delivery which I love as a description and will try to make more standard. I've also heard it called a "cannonball" delivery, which is equally fun.

If flexibility issues are stopping you from keeping the trailing leg extended through the slide, then the meatball delivery may be a workable variation for you. Some things to watch for are *when* the tuck happens and how it happens. Bringing that leg forward and under you is going to mean bringing the rock back as you shift your posture more upright (and also Newton's 3rd law*). If the tuck is happening close to the release point, it's going to be much harder to control the speed of the rock... though another downside is that if your knee or calf slides in that position, there will be *much* more drag than just a pointed toe, so your whole weight window will be very narrow even after you stabilize into the tuck. You may also twist off the line of delivery.

Broom Placement (for the Slide)

This is an area where you'll see a ton of variation. If we have the opportunity to play together you may even see me changing from shot to shot as I sometimes unconsciously go back to my old form of having my broom higher on my back and out more to the side vs. what I've been working on the past two years of keeping my broom head more in line with the rock, which puts the contact point on my back closer to my hip.

Some people slide with their brooms right down flat on the ice, even if they aren't a tuck thrower (see John Morris' delivery). Some float through the air, seemingly not needing a third point of contact on the ice at all – though that one I will say is an error and they should stop.

Some will have their brooms up over their shoulder (see Randy Ferbey's delivery). Some will wrap their arm around the broom.

And of course, some will have a stabilizer instead of a broom.

---

* "For every action there is an equal and opposite reaction" – bringing your trailing leg forward means everything else (i.e., the rock!) must be pulled back a bit to meet in the middle.

Whichever position you're using, remember the key points of the Curling Canada style positioning: it's to provide a source of balance and support, while keeping your shoulders square to the target and even when holding the rock with your other hand. If it's not helping you stay up in your slide, or making it hard to hit the broom because it's twisting your torso/shoulders, that's when it would be time to consider a change. If you're not able to find a way to use the broom to help hold you up, or if you're too tempted to use it as a balance beam in the air, perhaps try a few slides with a stabilizer instead.

Release Point

You'll see many pro curlers like to get fairly close to the hog line (where they *must* release) before releasing in their slide. This gives them the most time to fine-tune their line and feel their speed. They will also try to control their speed with their kick moreso than by altering the release point.

However, you may also see lots of people (especially at the club level) who may only slide as far as the near house and let it go, and that's fine too. The rock will curl slightly differently for the same broom position with different release points, but that's for the Skip to worry about (and as long as you're consistent with your release point, is relatively easy for them to adjust for you).

Some people may also have a neutral release, where they put the handle on without affecting the rock's speed or line, while others may have a more positive release, a slight arm extension that adds to the rock's speed and sets it out a bit from the broom.

However, if you're finding that you're *chucking* the rock at your release point, that may be time to reconsider your method. There's no need to slide way out to the hog line – just because that's where most pros release doesn't mean it's where *you* should try to get, especially if your shoes don't have really fast sliders on them to reduce that drag. If the right speed for you is at the near T-line, then by all means do your release there. There's not a lot of point in trying to slide further when you're going too slow and have to then push it to make up for that lost speed.

Summary

Anyway, there are lots of other potential variations on a delivery. My main point is that there's no single right way to throw a stone. The "Curling Canada" delivery is the way we teach it in learn-to-curl (and what I covered in the previous chapters), and there are reasons behind standardizing that way. However, lots of variant deliveries work just fine for getting stones in play and having fun. Your delivery will be unique to you, but hopefully all the ways that it is idiosyncratic are *working* for you. If a variation isn't there to serve your body or your style, then consider whether you want to try to bring it back to the "standard" Curling Canada style.

Sweeping/Brushing

Why we Sweep

How many times in this game have we had a rock that was just a few inches short of becoming shot, or making it by a guard, or staying straight enough to make a hit? Enough to know that sweeping **absolutely** makes the difference often enough that there is a good reason we have sweepers and don't just stand by and watch what happens.

It's a very important part of the game – indeed, other than the Skip, players will sweep more rocks than they throw. However, sweeping is wildly under-taught.

The slide and throwing in general is a unique physical challenge: it requires balance and flexibility and a lot of little parts coming together. And it's very different from any other daily activity. On top of that, it's pretty hard to get into the game without being able to throw a rock... so lots of reasons that the majority of the time that we have in learn-to-curl is spent focused on delivery.

It's a lot easier to get into the game and sweep kind-of-okay, but getting really good at sweeping is just as much effort as getting good at throwing rocks (even more so if you count getting in shape to sweep harder for longer). And it's when we start sweeping that curling becomes such a great way to exercise.

The most basic reason why we sweep is yes, to make shots, but moreover because it makes the **rock go straighter and the rock go further**.

Sweeping/Brushing

I heard that Glenn Gabriel* gets his Little Rocks to repeat that chant as a mantra when they go down the ice, and I haven't got our kids doing it yet, but really want to – in part because it sounds adorable and in part because it helps reinforce in their minds *why they are sweeping*.

I think many adults should do it for a while after learn-to-curl, too.

Yes, there's directional sweeping, and we'll get to that, but really the core of sweeping (and the traditional view of it before about a decade ago) was that the point of sweeping was to make the rock go straighter and make the rock go further. And for most of us at the club level, that continues to be the *entirety* of what sweeping is for.

Even a "light clean" helps with this: at the very least, you can stop a rock from picking (which really does make it go less straight and less far!). Even if you can't sweep fast or put a lot of weight over the brush head, you can help break up the frost and remove debris.

As for why sweeping works to help the rock go straighter and further (and possibly more, we'll get to directional sweeping soon enough), there are lots of theories that probably play together and explain part of the phenomenon. The problem is that physicists are not in agreement on how rocks curl at all in the first place, so there's some disagreement on the mechanisms involved in how sweeping works.

Removing debris and frost is not controversial. Less stuff for the rock to run into will help it travel further and more smoothly over the ice. This is pretty much a

---

* He runs the Little Rock program at East York Curling Club in Toronto, and also hosts the podcast *Coaching Kids Curling*, and was one of my instructors for my NCCP Club Coach certification.

baseline effect on top of the other potential mechanisms, and what even a light cleaning will help with.

Warming the ice is another mostly accepted theory – warmer ice will melt more easily, and may even have less friction with granite even if there isn't a *melted* layer of ice. The warmer ice theory doesn't allow for directional effects unless you have a gradient in the sweeping. But whatever, sweeping harder and faster (which helps generate more heat with the ice) should help make sweeping more effective based on this theory.

Polishing the pebble is another theory, that kind of runs counter to the next one, but still mostly works on the idea of making it easier for the rock to move down the ice.

Scratching the pebble is one theory behind why directional sweeping works – more aggressive pads (i.e., not the WCF-approved fabric used by pros and some competitive bonspiels these days, which was specifically created to reduce the effectiveness of this) can scratch the ice. For this to work, the scratches have to be aligned in certain directions to help make it easier for the rock to go in a certain direction (curl more, or run straighter and further).

Finally, a note on terminology: traditionally, we had "brooms" in curling, that we "swept" with. Our modern brooms look much less like those old corn brooms, and the motion much less like sweeping the floor, so many people are starting to call them "brushes" and the action "brushing".

They mean the same thing, it's just some newer terminology over some older ones. Personally I'm not such a huge fan of "brushing" simply because we already missed the boat on that – the horse hair brushes of the 90's would have fit that terminology *much* better than our modern foam-backed fabric brooms/brushes. Heck, a modern broom is closer to a **mop** than it is to either a broom or brush (and the home chore closest to the motions is also **mopping**), but I don't hear anyone pushing for that term (in small part because "mopping" is already taken as a verb in curling for what the icemaker does with the big 6'-wide mop after the game is over).

Whatever: you'll mostly see me say "broom" and "sweeping" because I'm old and those were the terms I grew up with. You'll see a lot of newer material refer to "brushes" and "brushing", but we're all talking about the same thing (and I'm not going to try to make a push to get "mopping" to stick as the verb, I can already see the *Mean Girls* "stop trying to make 'mopping' happen, it's not going to happen" meme).

KEEPING A BROOM DOWN

I mentioned "light clean" above, so it's perhaps a good time to talk about the basic terms.

When we have sweepers, we ideally want them sweeping with lots of pressure on the ice, lots of speed in the strokes, and of course, in front of the path of travel. But it's kind of exhausting to sweep so hard, and not every shot needs that. So if your Skip is yelling at the top of their lungs "yes, hard! Keep going!" then that's encouraging you to keep that effort up. Sweep hard by putting in that physical effort to put as much pressure and speed in as you can (*always* as *you* can – if you have to stop that's fine, no one is going to get mad if you need to catch your breath, it's just a game... but we'll encourage you as loudly as we can while you still have some gas in the tank).

But other times you may want to help the rock along with a little less vigour – that's where a "clean" comes in. The broom is down, you're clearing debris, but you're maybe not trying to get all your weight on it or moving it all that fast. There may not be much ice warming happening with a clean, but it can still help (indeed, a nearly-stationary "heavy clean" is becoming popular in the sport and is quite effective at helping rocks to go modestly further without being too energetically costly on the sweepers).

One thing we (and I very much include myself here) at the recreational level are not so good at is making use of that "clean" option in the brushing toolbox. For most reasonably close shots, we should probably be **keeping a broom down** for a light clean just to help reduce the odds of a pick. You'll sometimes hear people encourage this by yelling "just keep a broom down," though maybe you see that much more often on TV.

But more often you'll hear calls for regular/hard sweeping, or off, and very few for just cleaning.

TECHNIQUE

Similar to the delivery, there are a lot of little parts that make up a good sweeping form. Some of them are a little more intuitive than the parts of a delivery, but still worth some review.

Sweep in Front of the Rock

It's the simplest of tips: sweep in front of the rock to be effective. If you're a foot off to the side sweeping ice that the rock is never going to touch, then you're just wasting your effort and nothing else is going to matter.

Yet every few weeks I catch someone not sweeping in front of the rock. Sometimes it's late in the curl and they may not realize the rock is going almost sideways (so they may be sweeping between the rock and the backboards, which is *usually* what "in front of the rock" means, but that's not *currently* a patch of ice the rock will ever hit), but more often it's just simply a matter of not quite being in the right place with their broom.

The only part of the rock that touches the ice is the running band underneath. It's important to sweep the ice that this band will touch, so you don't quite have to sweep the entire width of the rock, though that's going to give you some margin of error. The running band is typically a bit smaller than the width of a brush head (see picture, below).

A small note is on "dumping" – while you want to sweep entirely in front of the rock, when you *stop* sweeping, you have to move your broom *out* of the path of the rock before lifting it off the ice. If you lift your broom straight up while still in front of the rock, you may "dump" debris in its path, which may slow the rock down, and is against the rules.

Clean Strokes

The broom goes one way, it comes back. You try to do it fast and with pressure on it, what could be simpler, right?

Unfortunately, many people will get more of a circular motion in their arms going rather than a straight, clean stroke. The broom looks like it's bouncing up and down on the ice as they go along, which is not as effective.

If the handle of your broom is changing its angle relative to the ice by a lot as you're sweeping, that's a good indication that your strokes are not clean and you're letting up the pressure at some point in the stroke. The cause is likely that instead of using the big muscles to lever and drive the broom, you're using the smaller muscles of your lower arm and wrist to manipulate the broom.

Use the Big Muscles

There are lots of ways to get your body to move a broom in front of a rock: you could, for example, wiggle it with your wrists. The reason why you probably *shouldn't* is that your wrists are not very strong: even an ultralight carbon fibre broom would tax the muscles driving your wrists after a game and you couldn't put much weight on the broom.

So you want to get your big muscles to do most of the work: your upper arm and shoulder muscles. Also, use your body weight to your advantage.

The way to do that involves holding your lower arm nearly straight: that arm is used mostly to help you get weight on the broom, and you need to keep that pressure up. The top arm has the elbow bent and will be doing much of the work in driving the broom back and forth, using the shoulder muscles and the triceps (big, strong muscles!).

If both elbows are moving during the sweep, you'll probably have a wiggly looking sweep and broom motion, and it likely means you're not getting much downward pressure on the broom head.

Open vs Closed

We teach "Open" stance in learn-to-curl for some very good reasons: you can look up more easily (to not trip over rocks in play) and the footwork is a lot easier (a shuffle with your feel pointing in the direction you're going).

Safety is always paramount, and for most players Open is the safer choice, and so a better default.

I myself only ever sweep Open, and can't for the life of me make my feet do the closed footwork dance, so you can be a modestly successful recreational curler using nothing but Open.

Anyway, let's take a step back, what is Open stance? What is Closed? It can be tough to relay just with words and some still pictures. But in essence, if you imagine standing to the thrower's left side, Open is when your right hand is down (i.e., the hand closer to the rock). That "opens" your chest to the target, so you can easily look up in the direction you're going. Closed is the opposite: if you're on the thrower's left, your left hand is down, so your chest is closed to the direction of travel and it's harder to see where you're going.

But these subtle shifts in which hand is down not only puts a different twist on your torso, it also changes where your hips point. I'm not the best model to use for form – I play a lot of Skip and not so much competitive front-end – but hopefully I'm good enough to get the points across in the picture below (here the rock is coming toward the camera).

Sweeping in Open position. Note that for this photo I am behind the rock and attempting to lean hard on my broom; standing more upright and more beside the rock is also fine at the recreational level (see next photo).

In Open, not only are you able to look up at the target, you can also (mostly) get your hips and feet to point in the direction of travel. This makes your footwork really easy: it's anything from a normal walk to a kind of cross-country-ski motion of shuffling your feet.

In Closed, not only is it hard to look up at the Skip (or other rocks that may be in the way), your hips are going to be twisted relative to the direction of motion, so you will have to adopt different footwork. That may be a side-to-side shuffle, or the intricate kick-back "C" motions that you'll see really good sweepers on TV use. This footwork is more complicated (and to repeat, not something I can do myself – you can be just fine at the club level only ever sweeping Open), and it's easier to trip yourself up as you're trying to learn that shuffle. When trying to put your upper body into Closed, it's natural to try to get your feet to walk backwards – obviously we don't want you doing *that* – proper footwork does require some practice.

So if Closed has all of these strikes against it, why mention it at all? For two reasons: first, if you prefer to have a certain hand down, then in order to switch sides you have to switch up your stance. But the bigger one is that you can put more weight on the broom in closed. Again, I'm not the best model for sweeping form (*waves in skip*), but even between these two pictures you can see that I'm able to drop my shoulders more in closed, get the broom closer to vertical, and put more downward force on the broom. Using the super-scientific bathroom scale method, I can put about 105 lbs of static force (less if I was actually on the ice and my feet had to be moving) in Open, and about 130 lbs in Closed – almost 25% more effective brushing, and I'm not even that good at Closed.

For 25%, a lot of front-end players will put the effort into learning the more complicated "C" footwork dance and trusting their partner to warn them of upcoming trip hazards (hopefully one of you is sweeping Open still).

Weight over the broom

Pretty much all theories of how sweeping works indicate that you are more effective with more pressure on the broom. When you have to start making trade-offs of pressure for speed it becomes a little more debated, but more pressure – given all else equal – is always helpful.

Part of that is going to be technique: working on getting your hands into the right place to let your back be straight and help transfer weight to the broom, to then using your feet to kick you up and over the broom head. Part of that is going to be about strength and fitness: if you're putting weight on the broom it means you are *holding yourself up by the broom* – a "sweeping plank" as

Stephanie Thompson of Empowered Performance* calls it.

So with good technique, you will be putting a lot of weight on the broom. That means you'll be relying on the broom to hold you up... which means if the broom is knocked out from under you, you *will* fall and maybe even break your face. Indeed, an accident just like that happened at our club a few years ago†.

Hopefully that's a good reminder that you should communicate with your other sweeper to be clear on who is going to be sweeping close to the rock and who will be sweeping further ahead so you don't smash brooms together.

Working Together...ish

Many pro teams are often only having one player sweep a rock, rather than both sweepers. This is in part for directional sweeping effects (which we'll get to) – they don't want the second sweeper coming in from the other side and counter-acting the directional effect they're after. But it's also in part because lots of research seems to agree that most of the effectiveness of sweeping comes from the first sweeper. The general consensus is that the first sweeper is doing about 80% of the work and the second sweeper who is further away is only at best adding about 20% to what the first sweeper has accomplished.

Sometimes you'll need every inch of that carry, but in other situations you may prefer to have a well-rested

---

* Indeed, I'll mention that Empowered Performance's specialty is making people "weapons on the ice" and she offers webinars and exercise programs to help improve fitness and technique for more effective sweeping. https://www.empoweredperformance.ca/

† https://thegrandslamofcurling.com/team-eppings-patrick-janssen-out-with-injury-after-fall-on-ice/

sweeper for your next shot, as well as someone who can keep their eyes up and help call the weight.

Skips Stay in the House

I had a lot of trouble with this personally: I *always* wanted to run out and help my sweepers as soon as I knew I was not going to call them off sweeping. In some cases, it can make sense: if a sweeper is flagging, you can rush in and relieve them so they can rest. But if you're not replacing someone, **adding a third sweeper does almost nothing to the rock**. Following that instinct to rush out to help sweep is depriving your team of someone to call line and possibly spot a plan B shot, with basically no benefit to the sweeping to show for it.

COMMUNICATION AND WEIGHT JUDGEMENT

There are lots of parts that go into being an effective sweeper: fitness, technique, equipment. But very little of that will matter if you don't know *when* to sweep.

The simplest answer is "when the Skip tells you to," but that is *very* incomplete: the Skip at the other end can see the line quite well, but it's *extremely* hard to tell how fast the rock is coming at you as a Skip, especially in the first half of the travel. It's up to the sweepers to make the call on how fast the rock is going, and then to communicate that up to the Skip.

So you have to start by taking a guess at how fast the rock is moving and where it will end up based on that. There are ways a stopwatch can help, but you should first develop a sense of that just using your eyes (and pace of your legs to keep up with the shot).

Letting the Skip know how heavy the rock is as it's moving down the sheet is important, because that is a big determinant in "calling the audible" – a rock that's the right weight may come by a guard just fine, while a heavy one might tick and change the call (and maybe if it's heavy you'll need to sweep to get that tick to slow it down).

There are lots of ways to communicate that, but the most common is to yell it up to the Skip. Don't worry, you'll be wrong a lot (I still am... a lot. A whole lot). You can (and will) change your mind as the rock goes down the ice and you get a better read on it.

Exactly what to yell can take many forms as well. Some teams use calls relative to the called shot (little light, right on, little hot, etc.), but I would prefer to teach some kind of absolute system. A common one used by competitive teams is the 10-point Ferbey system – if you hear someone yelling "four!" it's not a golfer with an errant ball you need to watch, it's someone calling for a rock to sit in the top 12' of the house. It's a good system in that it's pretty clear, widely used, and has short, distinct calls. However, it's overly specific for those of us at the club level – there's no meaningful difference between say a 5, 6, and a 7 that we can eyeball or time, so don't get too hung up on getting the exact right number if you decide to use it.

The Ferbey system uses three zones for guards. A "1" is from just over the hog line to about a third of the way through the guard zone, a "2" is the next zone for middle guards, and a "3" is for tight guards. Then each ring of the house gets a number: "4" for the top 12, through to "7" for T-line/button weight, and through to 10 for the back-12. "11" is sometimes called for a stone that will cross the backline.

Sweeping/Brushing

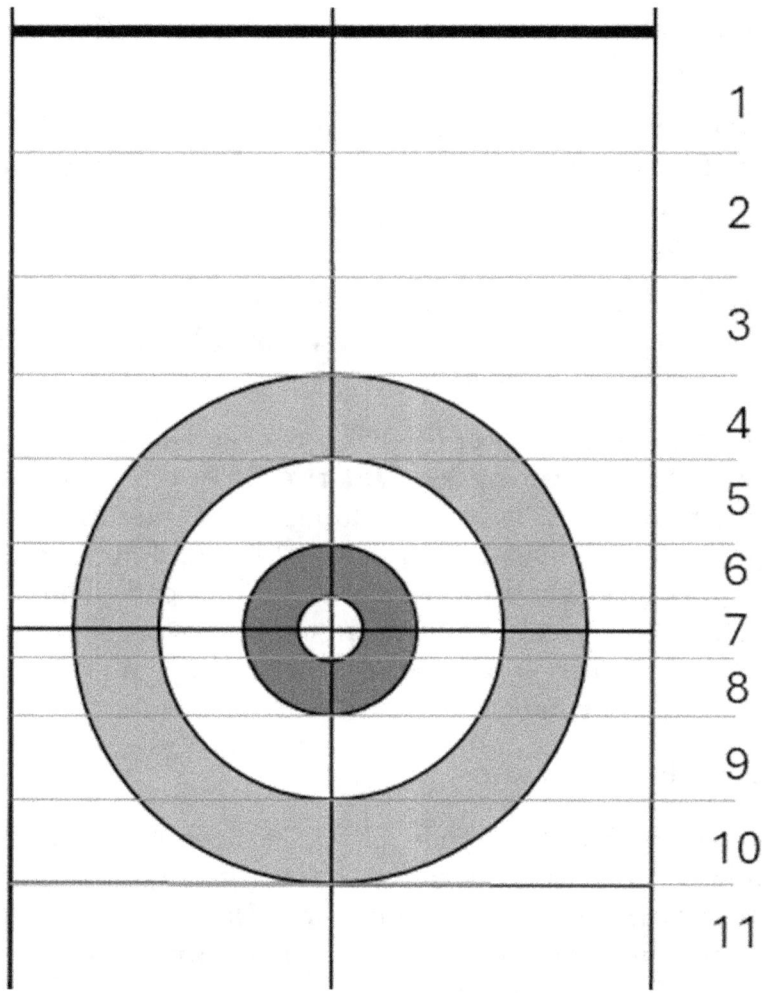

A simpler but just as effective system is to just call "guard", "in", or "through" – that's about as good as many of us will be able to judge it anyway, but also gives the Skip enough information to change the call if needed. If you're not up for yelling, you can use your hands to indicate, with a low/mid/high sign for either guard/draw/through if you like absolute signs, or light/close/heavy relative to the called shot.

Try to stick to one system for consistency and avoid confusing calls (tee-line and back-line are hard to distinguish in a noisy arena, as they both have "line", as is top-12/8/4 and back-12/8/4).

And again, you'll be wrong a lot, especially at first. But you'll get a better read on the ice (and your teammate's releases) and you can change your calls as the rock goes down the ice.

So once the Skip has the information on how fast the rock is going, they can yell down the sweep call (especially if the shot has now changed).

But if you see the rock is slow, you as the sweeper should start sweeping and let the Skip call you off (tell them that's why you're doing it). Generally the sweepers are the ones in charge of calling and managing the weight. The Skip may change the call or call them off for line, but if you think it's light you are generally empowered to start sweeping as you yell that down and let the Skip call you off.

Playing the Tolerance

We talked earlier about shot tolerance: for an open draw you may be targeting the top-4', but a little light (biting, even a guard) is still a good outcome. Depending on the situation, being even just a few feet heavy and giving the other team backing may be bad.

When you're in the role of sweeper, keep that shot tolerance in mind and sweep accordingly – if you want that top 4' draw, and if it looks like a good draw weight shot (say your best guess is top 8'), maybe give it a light clean but otherwise leave it alone until you're sure it's less than T-line when being light is a good miss.

Sometimes you have lots of tolerance to be heavy: that last rock of the end for instance, where the skipper just has to touch the 8' – and the back 8' works just as well as the top 8'. If you cannot be light and give up the steal, it may change how aggressively you start sweeping. If it looks like a pretty good draw, *just start sweeping*. Same thing if a shot has backing and looks close: the Skip may call you off for line (if it's really heavy it may go past the potential backing, for example), but if it's in the zone and the tolerance is to be heavier, you may want to start sweeping earlier.

DIRECTIONAL SWEEPING

Directional sweeping is the new hotness, so I bet you're glad I've finally wandered my way around to talking about it. However, it's also a little confusing. In part because it's really only about 10 years old, and in part because there isn't huge agreement on why it works so the techniques are still evolving.

If you aren't already at least a moderately effective sweeper, you will not be able to do directional sweeping. Even when trying to curl a rock, there's a good chance you will likely just straighten it and carry it further (though perhaps less than if you were sweeping specifically to straighten).

So a good idea is to book some practice ice (perhaps with some team members) and see which of these techniques work for you, if any, and if you're ever able to help a rock curl or if all you're ever doing is holding a rock straighter.

I want to repeat that part about there not being huge agreement on how it works – if you're able to make directional sweeping work for you in a way that isn't what I'm showing here, that's OK! I may be wrong. I'm interested in this stuff and have read a lot and experimented a bit, but there is lots of evolving information on ways to do directional sweeping and the physics underlying the effect(s).

High Side/Low Side

One set of terms you'll hear a lot when trying directional brushing is what we call the high side and the low side of the rock. Basically, which direction is *with* the curl and which is *against* it (or where is it curling from and where is it curling to)? The high side is the side where the rocks' rotation is moving that side in the direction of travel, so for a counter-clockwise turn, the right side (when looking from behind or above the rock as it moves, i.e. the usual sweeper perspective – which is why high and low can be useful terms, as the Skip's left/right is reversed from the sweepers').

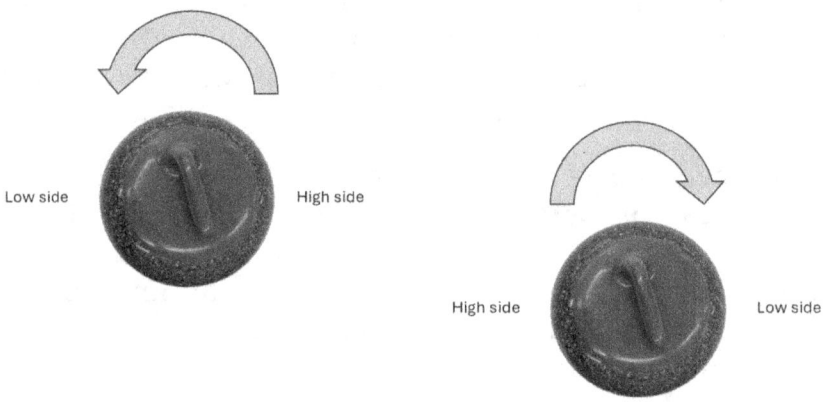

(In all of these figures, imagine the rock is moving from the bottom of the page to the top)

Approach 1: Scratch Theory

I'll cover this approach to directional sweeping first because it's the one that I find works for me and my technique/abilities.

The theory underlying this approach is that your broom makes small scratches in the ice that can help guide the rock. If scratches point toward the high side, it can help keep the rock straighter; if they point to the low side, they can help it curl more.

If you believe that scratches in the ice are what help guide the rock, then you want to **prioritize pressure** over broom head speed and aren't too fussed about long strokes that get the head of your broom a little bit away from the rock.

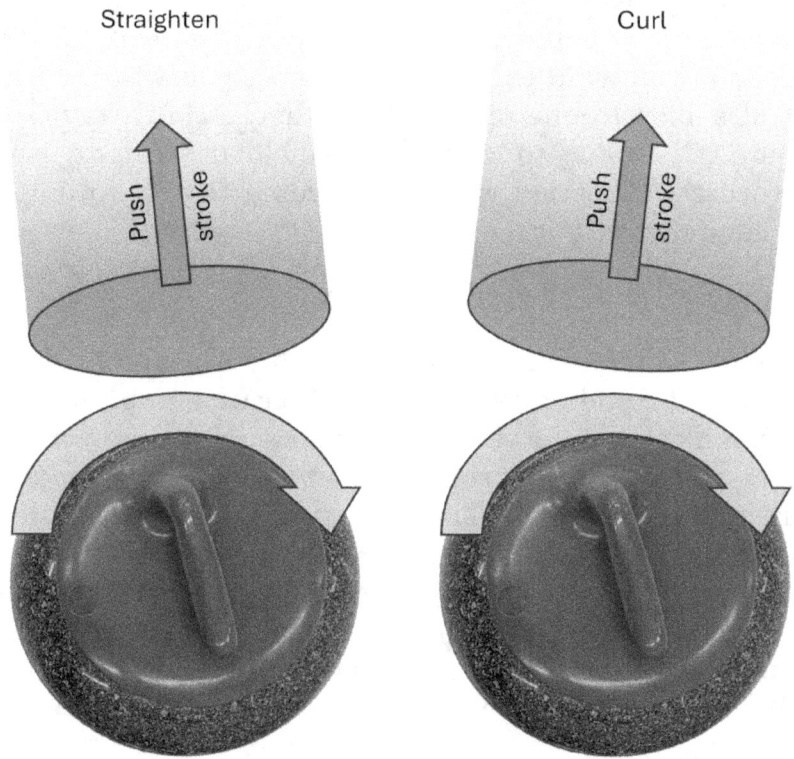

(And of course mirror that image for the opposite turn)

A key part of this approach is going to be your broom's push angle: you will want to be sweeping so your broom is mostly aligned with the direction of travel of the stone, off by 10–30° to either the high or low side for holding the stone straight or adding curl. To do that, you'll have to position your feet behind the rock, and lean over it to get your broom's head in front of the rock. So the sweeper standing on the low side (for a clockwise rotating rock, the person on the right) would sweep toward the high side to help increase curl (against the direction it's curling). And then the opposite to promote curl: the sweeper standing on the high side (for a clockwise rotating rock, the person on the left) would sweep toward the low side to help increase curl.

In other words, for the scratch theory approach to directional sweeping, you'll basically sweep in the direction you want the rock to go: mostly forward, with a bit of a bias to one side or the other. A bit away from where it is going to curl to help hold it straight, a bit toward the direction where it is going to curl to help it curl more.

Approach 2: Gradient Theory

A quick history break: after brooms with more durable fabric that could make these small scratches on the ice to enable directional sweeping came out (Hardline was the first), the curling world was seized by the scandal of directional sweeping*. The different materials could lead to an unfair advantage (or the *perception* of an unfair advantage), and so the players and manufacturers got together to agree on a single standardized fabric to use in brush heads for high-level competitions. This is now called the World Curling Federation (WCF) fabric.

The WCF fabric is (always) mustard yellow, and was chosen specifically to not scratch the ice as much. However, many teams still believe that the directional sweeping method from the last section works for them with WCF-compliant brooms. We can either believe that

---

* John Cullen has a 6-part podcast covering that time period: https://www.cbc.ca/listen/cbc-podcasts/1427-broomgate-a-curling-scandal

the WCF fabric is only partially effective at eliminating scratches, or decide that another theory of directional sweeping is needed.

Indeed, before scratch theory people talked about "corner sweeping." Now there's a revitalization of the thinking that a *gradient* in the warming of the ice affects the curl.

If you believe that heating the ice is the main effect, and directionality comes from a *gradient* in that heat, then you want to prioritize a **combination of pressure and broom head speed** to maximize your heat generated (i.e., **total power output** vs pressure). You also want to stay closer to the rock in your movements.

There's a differential in force between your push and pull stroke, but more importantly both get weaker further from your start point (when the sweeper can put the most weight on the broom).

Glenn Paulley published* some data on the difference in force between the push and pull stroke, and between the starting position (when the sweeper can put the most weight on the broom) and the end of the stroke.

So you want that push stroke to go in the direction you want the rock to go (i.e., sweep from the high side to get it to curl, from the low side to hold it straight). This is the same sweeper selection as with approach 1. The angle of attack that you would use is then going to be more perpendicular to the direction of travel than with the scratch-theory-based approach: now you want to have more of a high-side-to-low-side difference, which you don't get much of when "snowplowing" like before. So you may aim for something like 45-60°. But you're still calling for the same person to hold the line vs curl.

---

* https://glennpaulley.ca/curling/2024/02/14/the-anatomy-of-a-brush-stroke/

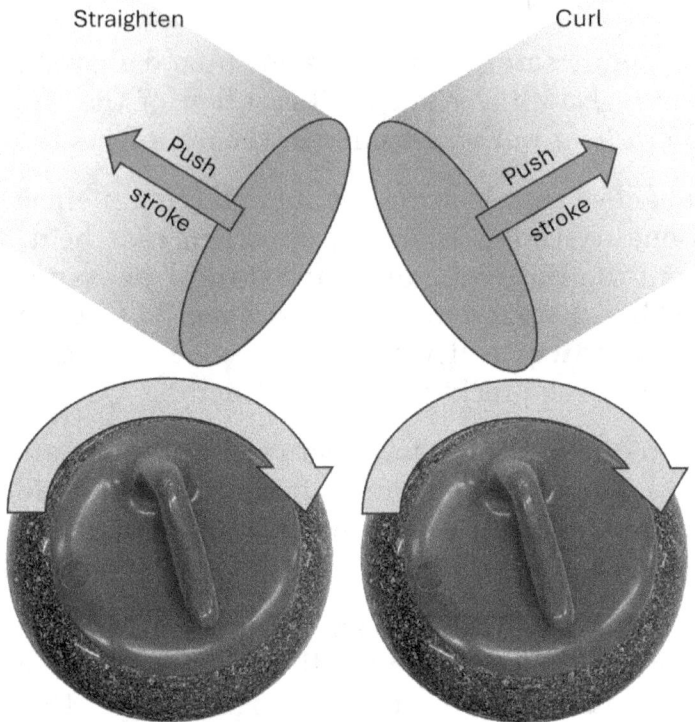

Approach 3: Knifing

Building on the idea of having a gradient of heating across the face of the rock to influence the curl, there is a thought that the gradient is even stronger if your stroke does not quite cover the full width of the running band. One way to do that is to hold your broom with the skinny edge going in the direction of the stone.

A modification is to use your broom like that but *sweep enough to cover the full running surface* (to help protect against picks). Even then the gradient in heating will be much larger than before: the end of the stroke for the low side is going to finish well in front of the rock, producing very little heating compared to the high side. This is a much larger gradient in heating than you get with your broom as a "T" and sweeping at 30-45° to the direction of travel.

Note that I only have one version of the figure here because my understanding is that knifing for holding the line is practically never used – this technique is almost exclusively for trying to add curl, possibly without adding carry. To keep the rock straight, you'd generally use either a snowplow-type technique sweeping from low to high, or get both sweepers involved. Though I suppose in theory if you wanted to keep a rock straight *without* adding to the carry you could try knifing in the direction to hold it straight. That's going to be a unique benefit of the knifing approach – all the other methods are in theory going to carry the rock further while holding it straight.

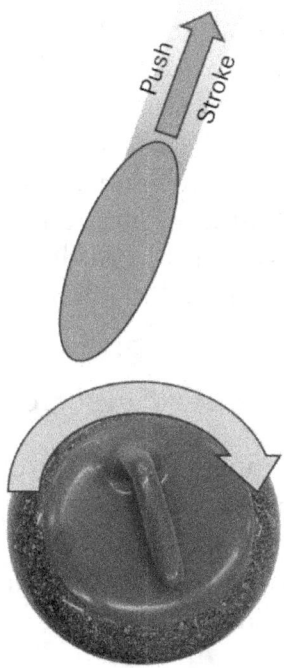

I've had limited success trying the knifing approach in practice sessions. In part it may be that with the recreational fabric, the first approach (which relies on scratch theory) is simply more effective, or it may be an interaction between the techniques and my particular abilities and techniques. However, only a few pro teams are using the knifing method at the moment, so it is something that's still evolving.

A downside of knifing is that you have to be even more precise with your broom placement: it is very easy to find yourself mostly sweeping outside the path of the running band, and you don't have much in the way of margins like the other techniques do. That is, if your broom head is already ~1-2" longer than the running band is wide, and you're moving it at least a few inches side to side because you're not sweeping perfectly in line with the direction of travel, then you've got a bit of margin on either side of the running band. So if you found yourself drifting off a few inches one way or the other, you're still getting coverage. With knifing, you're now aligning the skinny side of your broom to the direction of travel, so your base coverage is now only about half the width of the running band. Plus you may not have as much horizontal movement in the knifing strokes, so being a few inches off in your original placement may cause you to not do any effective work at all as you entirely miss the path the running band is going to hit.

"Approach" 4: Sweeper Selection

I am putting scare quotes here as I don't believe that the people using this approach are actually accomplishing directional brushing – I think they are in most cases making the rock go straighter and further (as with our Little Rock mantra).

Anyway, this technique basically uses just one sweeper as with the others, choosing the sweeper on the low or high side for holding line or curling as with the other techniques, *but with no adjustment in the actual sweeping method*: the sweeper is sweeping across the face of the rock perpendicular to the direction of travel, what I might call "regular sweeping 2007 style," especially if they have the thin edge of the broom perpendicular to the direction of travel.

There are good reasons to sweep this way, and indeed our modern broom heads owe their swivel designs to this theory: with a wider broom head, you are always covering the path to pick up debris and reduce picks, rather than having your broom zig-zag across the ice and possibly miss patches. With good sweepers who coordinate well enough to not bang into each other's brooms, you could get two people sweeping in the space one old-fashioned broom would take, increasing the heating/carry for the stone by virtue of being able to get in closer to the running band (and hopefully exceeding that accepted 20% extra effectiveness figure for the 2nd sweeper).

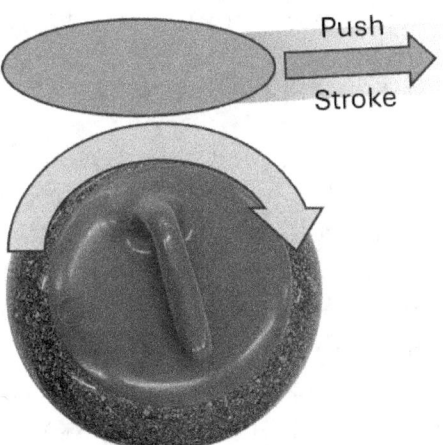

However, there is no gradient across the high to low side of the rock that should be affecting the curl, so this *shouldn't* work as a directional approach.

If anybody uses this method with their team and tested it somewhat rigorously and found that it *actually* does help to curl the rock (not just hold it more or less well) I'd be interested in hearing more.

A Quick Directional Sweeping Demonstration

I think it's important to test out whether you are able to make directional sweeping work at all for you, and how much of an effect you're able to have with your technique, broom, ice conditions, etc. That can help you deploy it best, and also determine if it's worth all the hassle in the first place.

But there aren't a lot of demonstrations of how effective directional sweeping can be, so here are a set of rocks from a practice session at Unionville Curling Club in Ontario. I enlisted the help of DZ, a competitive junior curler in our club, using a broom with a recreational cover (i.e., one where the approach based on scratch theory should work). His draw weight is more consistent than mine, but for this particular test we weren't super controlled (I didn't time the rocks to confirm they were similar out of his hand before sweeping effects kicked in).

We found that sweeping for curl carried the rock a tiny bit further and it curled about a half a rock more than it did otherwise. One held for line (and also carry) went about 8' further and curled about half a rock width less. That's pretty typical from what I've found in my practices – I can get roughly half a rock to a rock width of difference in the amount of curl one way or the other, and about 4–8' of extra carry. Your mileage may vary. But those results are enough to make or break many shots in the game.

A Reminder for Club Play and In Which I Immediately Contradict Myself

Finally, I'll close this out by saying that many of us likely are not going to be effective at getting a rock to curl more with sweeping. Most of our sweeping efforts are going to be of the traditional "the rock goes straighter, the rock goes further" variety. So it's totally fine to ignore all this and have your sweeping calls simply be on or off. Even if your sweepers *can* do directional sweeping, it is an extra step to coordinate the calls.

And to contradict myself there, while many of us are not at the level the pros are at in terms of being able to put weight on the broom or put out total power, we have an equipment advantage: we don't have to use the WCF-approved fabric in club play, so you can be a moderately effective sweeper and still accomplish some directional sweeping.

Either way, it's not necessarily a bad idea to keep in mind. Even if you just want to keep the rock straight, you may want to make sure that the person on the low side to hold the line straighter is closer to the rock so you don't accidentally get a minor directional effect that's countering your sweep call. After all, while the effects may be small for many of us, sometimes a quarter inch or less is all that stands between making a sweet come-around or wrecking on a guard. That is, even small effects sometimes matter in a game.

If you do want to become a weapon on the ice, you'll need to be able to put downward pressure on the broom (form & strength) and/or have higher power (in Watts, pressure and speed combined). And that may require some off-ice training and fitness work.

Playing Together

Safety

As a non-contact sport played by people as young as 7 (and a few notable examples of curlers starting even younger) and right into their 80's and 90's, curling has a well-deserved reputation as a pretty safe sport. However, it is played on ice.

Ice is hard and slippery, and moreover *unforgiving*. Accidents can and do happen, and it behooves us to do what we can to make things as safe as possible.

Just like winter driving, you want to try to **limit your rate of acceleration or deceleration** on the ice: speed up slowly, slow down slowly (where possible). The one time we want to accelerate explosively is when delivering a stone, and for that we get to start on the hack, our one little island of high-grip rubber. Everywhere else, give yourself some space and time to speed up or come to a stop.

If you're sweeping, you don't have to start at the hog line: start a little further in and accelerate as your thrower is sliding, so that you're up to speed by the time they release before the near hog line. If you're the one delivering the stone, take a few seconds to slow down after release: follow-through on your slide to slow down for a bit before trying to stand; if you're a stick thrower, keep walking after releasing the rock and take a few steps to come to a stop. (Indeed, in a podcast* Bill Tschirhart shared that stick curlers trying to come to a sudden stop after release

---

* https://www.buzzsprout.com/1922969/11544006 *A Pane in the Glass*: "How Much is Your Brain Worth?"

is a surprisingly frequent source of falls, especially the worst kind, where you fall backward from standing).

When stepping on or off the ice, step *between* the rocks, not over them, and always on your gripper foot (so for righties, right foot first). Even if you have two grippers on *that time*, it's best to get into that habit of always stepping down gripper-foot first for the time when you have your slider exposed.

A rock can have a lot more momentum than your gripper has grip on the ice, so wild rocks can very easily take a person down. Be sure to catch rocks (ideally with your broom, but with your foot if need be), especially if they're going sideways after a hit onto a neighbouring sheet where a player may be watching their own play and not rocks coming from behind or from the flanks. While Skips (or Vices) in the house are usually the first line of defense and the ones to say when a rock is out of play, **anyone on the ice is empowered to stop a rock before it becomes a hazard**, especially if it is crossing the sideline to another sheet where the players may not be looking out for it.

Again, similar to driving, your rubber (gripper or tire) will only have so much traction with the ice. Things go much, much better when you stay within that traction limit than when you get outside of it and start to slide. Try to keep your weight directly over your grippers when walking – large steps where more of your force comes at an angle increases the likelihood that your grippers will slide. And if things are getting too fast for you, keep to your safe speed (if someone is throwing peel and you're not comfortable chasing it to sweep, let it go).

And finally, if you can't avoid a fall, try to minimize the damage.

That can include protective gear. Though no headband or helmet can promise to eliminate the risk of a concussion, a general principle is that something between your head and the ice is going to be better than nothing. If you're going with a headband or hat type solution, it has to be **tight**, and/or have a chinstrap. If you do fall, you want it to actually stay on your head to be there between your head and the ice – it does you no good if it's flying off mid-fall. For that reason, some people recommend that you only use something with a chinstrap.

The other way to minimize the damage is to fall better. Falling forward, you're more likely to cushion things with your arms than falling backward. Falling from standing is going to be a bigger hit than falling from a lower position. That's something they cover in learn to curl: **if you're losing your balance in the slide, go down from the slide position**. It hurts so much less to just roll to the ice when you're already most of the way down than to try to get to your feet while you're unstable and wobbling, and *then* fall. Yet it's a natural enough instinct – the curling delivery position is a weird one we're not normally in, but we feel comfortable standing, so when off balance we try to get back to standing as soon as possible. Fight that instinct and stay down for a second, whether that's putting your knees on the ice (not a good habit to get into for every delivery, but again better than a fall) or rolling flat out onto the ice. Get up slowly – yes, hand and knee prints are the curler's bane, but take a second to be sure you're getting that gripper foot under you before you get back up. Safety comes before worrying about the icemaker's ire.

ON-ICE COMMUNICATION

Communication. That can mean a lot of things, particularly for teams that play a lot of events together, but here I'll talk about on-ice communication. If you listen to the commentators for the Brier or Scotties, they love to praise teams with good communication, and that's because it is important, and takes a little effort to do well consistently.

The sheets are long and the rink is loud, so most communication between the Skips and throwers is in the form of gestures (sometimes we yell, but rarely successfully). Tapping the ice for where a shot should end up (possibly a few taps/gestures for the tolerance), followed by holding the broom for a target with a hand up to indicate the curl is the most basic communication from Skip to thrower, and hopefully pretty well covered in your learn to curl (if not, be sure to read the section on playing back end).

But you may have seen a few other signs: a take-out often involves tapping a rock then flicking the broom a bit. Then accompanied by some sign for the weight to throw.

That's a little less standard, but most often for a hack weight shot (where you throw hard enough to stop at the hack at the other end – a few feet more than it needs to just sail through the backline, only a little heavier than a draw) a Skip will either tap their shoe, or point their broom at the hack behind them (in some cases, walking back to tap it).

For a board weight hit (a little more than hack – enough to get to the back boards with maybe a little bounce, a "just noticeable difference" heavier than hack), some common signs include waving the broom behind but higher (pointing at the back wall), pointing at the side wall, or tapping their hip.

Tapping a rock then holding the broom up horizontally is the sign for a "tap" or "raise" shot. The Skip will often then slide their broom back and forth across the house at the weight they want the thrower to use, back 8 for example.

Curling for Beginners and Improvers

That's the general pattern:

1. Signal for desired outcome
2. Signal for desired weight, if needed to specify (not so much for the guards and draws where you're tapping where you want it to end up so the weight information is contained in the outcome call)
3. Planting broom and holding arm up for line and handle, respectively.

Communication going the other way is also important, and the one that's a little harder to remember to do.

Letting the Skip know how heavy the rock is as it's moving down the sheet is important, because it's really hard to tell from the Skip's vantage point, especially soon after release. Yet knowing the weight is critical to knowing how to manage the line and what "Plan B" the Skip may have to cook up.

There are lots of ways to communicate that, from simple signs to whole conversations about what you think the weight might do, your opinion of the path, how much distance you think you can add if you started sweeping...

Playing Together

but the most common is to yell a short, simple weight call up to the Skip.

Exactly what to yell can take many forms as well. Some teams use calls relative to the called shot (little light, right on, little hot, etc.), but there are advantages to using an absolute system. Not the least of which is that if the sweepers mis-interpret the called shot, the information given back up to the Skip isn't tainted by that.

A common absolute weight calling system used by competitive teams is the 10-point Ferbey system – see the previous section on sweeping for details on that. To reiterate, it's a common system that's simple which makes it a decent overall choice and default to turn to, but it's also over-specified for those of us at the club level. Don't get too hung up on getting the exact right number, and free to call out ranges "3-4" "8-10" to avoid the false precision.

A simpler but just as effective system is to just call "guard," "in," or "through" – that's about as good as many us will be able to call it anyway, but also gives the Skip enough information to change the call if needed.

Making the guesses is also important to improving your own ability to guess. To break out the pop psychology, committing to your guess and having to (audibly, in front of other people) change your mind and admit you were wrong forces your brain to pay more attention to the guess and the correction than if you were to try the same thing silently in your head until you felt like you were "good enough" at weight judgement to start guessing out loud. Making those mistakes while it's still very socially acceptable to not be correct (indeed, to be expected to get it wrong more often than not) also helps during the learning process, rather than waiting until you should be able to call weight to actually do so.

Curling for Beginners and Improvers

You can also come up with your own zone system with your team. I suggest avoiding numbers – the Ferbey system has a pretty strong monopoly on those and it would just be more confusing. But if you want to simplify things to 4 or 5 zones you could use some other system that's clear to you. For example, you could use animal names, like hog/turtle/horse/rabbit; if you're playing with different people each week something universal is nice, like guard/top house/deep/through.

SPEED OF PLAY

Curling ice time is typically in short supply. Leagues only have so much time to complete a game, so to get as many ends in as possible, it's up to everyone out there to keep things moving.

If you get a 2-hour timeslot for your game, the difference between fitting 8 ends in and only getting 7 is just being 8 seconds per rock slower.

To play faster is mostly about being ready to play to eliminate dead time. As soon as the other team has released their rock, you are allowed to start moving your rock to the hack, clean it, take your gripper off, etc., so that you are ready to throw as soon as your Skip puts the broom down. You don't have to stand there and watch the other team's rock the whole way down, and only after it stops start thinking about getting ready for your shot.

As a Skip, thinking ahead about what you might do if the other team makes their shot or misses in a certain way will help you step in and put the broom down just about as soon as the rocks stop moving.

Playing fast most of the time will help build some slack time for the odd shot where the Skip does need to think about it, or consult with the other players. Or for the odd time that a player forgets their delivery device at the other end.

STAYING OUT OF THE WAY

As a courtesy, we don't want to interfere with the other team's shot. That means that when you're a sweeper and walking back from the scoring end to the delivery end, you should do so near the edges of the sheet.

As sweepers, you'll stay between the two hog lines while the other team is throwing (or preparing to throw), staying out of everyone's way.

We don't want to cause a visual distraction for a thrower, so if for some reason we do have to move behind the house (as the opposing Skip/Vice, or just to wipe debris off your broom or grab a facial tissue or some water), pause when the thrower is in their slide. If you have to run off the ice (e.g., to visit the toilets), keep that same principle in mind for all the other sheets, and pause before crossing a sheet when someone is throwing.

As the Skip (or Vice in the house) of the non-throwing team, we often want to watch the line of delivery. It's acceptable to try to position yourself behind the Skip/Vice holding the broom to watch the line, but if you do so, stand still. Don't put your broom down on the ice to cause a visual distraction or confusing target. Personally, I find it's hard enough to see over most other Skips' shoulders that I wait behind the house and off to the side until the thrower has released, then slide in to be able to bob my head back and forth to try to get a read on the line if I can't look directly down it due to the other Skip's opacity.

For the most part, limit the people on the backboards. Many of us want to wait on the backboard after our team is done, but it can add extra pressure to the hammer team's Skip's last shot if the entire opposition is stacked up behind the house. Generally, the Leads and Seconds should wait between the hog lines even for the last few rocks, even when their team is all out of rocks. If there's a reason to be back there (e.g., to limit the time spent standing on slippery ice, to get some water, blow their nose, or wipe a broom off into the trash bin, head for the edges of the sheet rather than the middle (and ideally, the one opposite the target of the shot in progress).

UNWRITTEN RULES

Building upon our earlier discussion of the Spirt of Curling and the culture that can surround a sport, let's attempt to write down some of the many unwritten rules that help govern the sport.

Speed of play: try to play fast (be ready as the thrower, make a call quickly as a Skip – see the section earlier on tips for speed of play), and be understanding those few times when the other team needs to be slow (the call is hard and the Skip needs to talk it out, or the thrower forgot their delivery device at the other end in an honest mistake).

Displays of Anger/Frustration: We all get frustrated sometimes, largely at ourselves (or that pick!), but expressing that *maturely* is important – we don't bang our brooms on the backboards for that satisfying boom to echo our mood (though I believe shaking our fists at the rafters is still considered acceptable).

Queuing Rocks: A fairly standard practice is for a team's Lead to grab the Skip's stone and place it in the hack while the Skip and Vice are at the other end deciding on the call. That helps speed the game up a tiny bit, but no one will think you rude if you didn't know that/forgot to do it. It used to be more common (or a regional thing in London) to queue up the other team's stone beside the hack, up and down the lineup, however it's a mostly empty display: people were still having to move *a* rock from the backboard to the hack on their turn, and there was an extra tripping hazard in a weird place. And if you were running behind, it made the pace of play even slower, so it's not typically done now (and discouraged by many league convenors). Still, you may find that it's a tradition at some clubs, and if so, feel free to participate (and get those rocks moving early enough to keep the pace of play up).

Off-Ice Culture

A lot of the more confusing parts of curling culture come off the ice, and I'm perhaps not the best person to attempt a guide to it because I've been steeped in that culture a long time.

Broomstacking: Stacking your brooms up in the corner (figuratively) and sitting down to share a drink (largely literally but also sometimes figuratively) with the opposition is a big part of curling culture[*]. A tradition is for the winning team to buy the losing team a drink of their choice. The losing team then will usually feel an obligation to reciprocate and buy a second round for the winning team (and themselves). And while often we don't have people drinking two rounds after many of our leagues, and the winners will often graciously deny that they are still thirsty, it's important as the losing team who just got to drink for free *to offer* (whether it's important to then decline the second round is very non-standardized).

---

[*] At least in Ontario. People reading this draft told me it's not as common in Western Canada.

Now, we have to balance that tradition with the reality that we are not farmers in the 50's hoping the winter goes by faster. We have things to do and there's only so much time in a week you can devote to curling (and even within the time to devote to curling, the cold hard math says that cutting a half hour off of broomstacking from four leagues/week lets you add a fifth league...). However, there are still some traditionalists who will worry if you're running out because you thought they were a bad sport about something and don't want to hang with them. Or wonder if *you're* being a bad sport and running off without the broomstacking bit because you're a sore loser/winner. So be sure to give those excuses: "I have to relieve the babysitter/the dogs need a walk/I need to be at work early in the morning/now that I'm limbered up I have to run home to do sex to my partner/I still have a weekly email tip to write" or if you're very, very lucky "I have to get back out on the ice for another game!" to make it clear that you're not running out because of something that happened on the ice.

It's also important to recognize that some people have very good personal reasons for not wanting to drink, and potentially not wanting to buy a drink (particularly an alcoholic one) for someone else. The tradition is a bit too entrenched to wave a magic wand and do away with entirely (but just in case: *from the date of publication of this book onward, everyone shall buy their own drinks!* ...eh, worth a try), but we should be compassionate and understand that not everyone will want to buy for reasons that may be their own (whether religious prohibitions, personal demons with alcohol, or other). I think in my ideal world, everyone would be comfortable enough with each other to just say so: "Hey, great game, can I get you a drink?" "Sure, make it a beer." "Oh, do you mind if we make it a non-alcoholic option for this round?" "Of course not! Coke Zero in that case, thanks!"

That kind of thing requires a lot of trust that everyone will be OK with a slight bending of tradition in that way, and moreover trust that they won't feel othered simply for making the request. Instead, we may have to accept that some people may run off after the game without buying a round. We should be careful not to think that they are being bad sports but rather consider that they may be trying to avoid an awkward conversation about their reasons for avoiding alcohol (or have other responsibilities that call them away).

Volunteering: Curling clubs only survive thanks to the efforts of many volunteers. Organizing spiels, and leagues, and ice time is typically all volunteer-driven. And every event needs a small army of volunteers, from making signs to moving chairs, to plating snacks.

It's a lot of work, but it's also intrinsically rewarding. If you haven't yet volunteered for something, put your hand up the next time a call for volunteers comes around and give it a whirl. It's not that hard, it's not that scary, and everyone is super nice.

The truism of "many hands makes light work" holds for many tasks in running a curling event. For a recent spiel I volunteered to be on the committee, and had very little work to do personally. We created a job list, with a lot of tasks:

- Determine rules, format, prizes, etc.
- Solicit sponsorships
- Buy prizes (or decide to use cash, then handle cash)
- Determine snacks menu
- Buy snacks
- Serve snacks
- Get quotes from caterers/restaurants for dinner
- Determine dinner option
- Arrange catering
- Service and cleanup from dinners

- Setting up and taking down (e.g., moving dinner tables to lounge and back)
- Master of ceremonies for each night
- Drawmaster/scorekeeper
- Photos/social media
- Devise budget
- Registration
- On-site experts to explain rules, officiate if need be
- Accept registrations (email)
- Create poster
- Print/hang posters
- Draft email announcement

That is an overwhelming amount of stuff for one person to handle. But with six of us chipping in, it's just three or four very manageable tasks each.

Sparing: You can field a team with three players, indeed sometimes you may prefer that so you can get some more rock throwing practice in. But if you know one player is going to be away, and you don't get a spare, and another player has a surprise last-minute reason to miss (like catching covid) then suddenly you've forfeited. So we generally always try to find a spare.

And, especially in these times after covid, we try to find a spare liberally. Just don't come when you're sick, even just a little sick.

In some leagues, they have various rules about who can spare, with a kind of hierarchy of who to look for. Those rules are basically aimed at trying to avoid the perception of having gone and got a ringer – if your Lead is away, you wouldn't typically find someone who's an ace at Skip and then let them call the game for you. Even if you got a "better" player, they'd still play at or below the position of the person they're replacing in most leagues. (Though the specific rules will vary depending on your specific club/league.)

So, you start with people "at your level", but if you can't find someone, you're usually free to widen the circle until you do – for example in Mixed Doubles we prefer to replace a player with someone of the same sex so the team is still mixed, but c'mon, it's a situation where you needed a spare in the first place. If a team is temporarily two people of the same sex no one is going to care that much (especially in a casual/social league). In our Mixed league they're a little more strict about position/experience matching – I'd be willing to spare at any position any time, but they only want me sparing for Skips and would rather a team run with three than have me show up to spare at Lead.

I'm Surely Missing More

And of course, one of the problems of being someone who started curling as a kid is that I'm fairly deeply steeped in a lot of this Spirit of Curling stuff, so a lot of it seems like "the natural way the world should be" and is thus invisible to me. On the chances that this book ever sees a second edition in the future, please feel free to send me any unwritten rules I've missed, or weird curling culture idiosyncrasies you think newbies need to be prepared for.

KEEPING THE ICE CLEAN

No, this isn't a rehash of sweeping, instead it's about avoiding debris in the first place.

Curling ice is kind of a magical surface. The icemaking team puts a lot of effort into ensuring a good playing surface, which involves scraping to flatten and refresh the surface, pebbling to get that texture for curl to happen, and nipping those pebbles for even more consistency. And all of that can be undone by a tiny piece of debris causing a pick.

So it behooves us to respect the ice and do what we can to keep it clean.

Footwear & Grippers

The biggest factor there is our shoes. Even if you don't have a pair of purpose-made curling shoes, you should have a pair of *dedicated* shoes – perhaps a pair of runners that after the season ends in April will become your daily trainers for the year, but for now are kept pristine and clean for curling.

Tracking in salt and sand is perhaps the worst possible thing for the ice, so as the weather gets bad remember to go straight from outside to the locker rooms, lose those outdoor boots, and put on your curling shoes.

Even with clean shoes, you'll find a lot of the gunk on the ice is in the form of little black rubber dots. That comes from our grippers breaking down. Grippers are a wear item (in the sense that they wear out and need to be regularly replaced). The tread on grippers will gradually wear away (that fingerprint texture will start to look smooth), which is a safety reason to replace them. But they also get weak from being stretched to go on and off several times a game, and will start dropping bits of rubber. The rough rule of thumb is that you need to replace a gripper every year for every day of the week you play. So if I'm in three leagues, I'll go through about three grippers in a year (i.e., I change my gripper every two months). If you only play once a week, you'll likely want to start each year with a new set of grippers*.

You should also clean your gripper periodically. At some clubs you may notice sticky sheets that you step on as you

---

* This is why, at least at our club, you can borrow brooms, sliders, and stabilizers as a newbie until you sort out your own, but have to buy your own grippers – they wear out too fast to lend out.

go into the ice shed to help clean the bottoms of your shoes/grippers. You can use the same principle at home: take a piece of tape every now and then and get the dust and rubber debris off of your gripper. A good idea is also to do it to the **inside** of your gripper, which can start to look debris-filled (and transfer gunk to your slider) long before the gripper itself needs to be replaced.

Brooms

We use our brooms to clean the path in front of the stone. Sometimes, we'll have visible evidence of that effort in the form of debris on the broom.

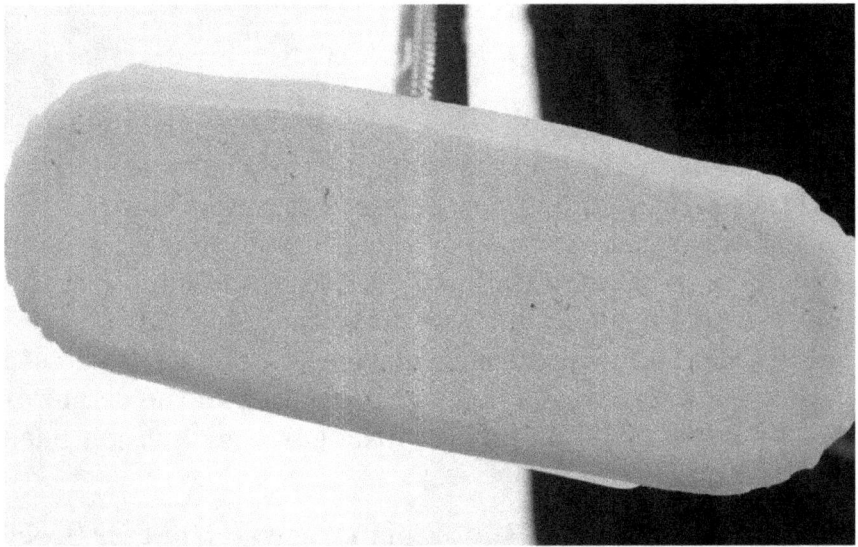

The point is not just to move the debris from one part of the ice to another, so head over to a garbage can and brush that crud off your broom and into the bin. You'll likely find you need to do that at least every end (depending very much on how much you're sweeping and how clean the ice is to start).

Even with regular swipes to get rid of most debris, you'll see your brush head getting clogged up with debris over time. Some heads have been specifically designed to be washable (e.g., the recreational version of the hardline cover), so go ahead and wash them from time to time.

Even then (especially if you have an older-style broom that doesn't make for easily washing), the heads are another wear item. They will likely last a little longer than grippers, but a similar rule-of-thumb is in play: you'll likely need at least one new one each year, maybe more if you play a lot (I mostly Skip so my broom is really only seeing heavy use the one day/week I play doubles, so I can get through a year with just ~2 broom heads, but have to wash each one 3–4 times in that period; it would easily be 2–4 pad replacements if I played front end for three nights/week).

Other Sources of Debris

Not everyone is as blessed as I am with the natural adaptation to the sport of curling that is male pattern baldness. Hair can be a big source of picks, however it's one that we just have to learn to live with (I am *not* going to tell those of you with lovely full heads of hair that you have to cover it up just to play, though it is a minor additional bonus to choosing to wear a helmet). If you see a piece of hair, there's no need to try to find the owner or get all icked out, just put it in the garbage, and get back to the game.

Clothing can also be a source of picks: watch out for fleecy sweaters, track pants, or even mittens that like to shed tiny fluff balls.

Timing Rocks

In curling most technology is banned – quiet Skips like me can't use a megaphone, and we can't use a LIDAR system to map out imperfections in the ice. The one piece of technology that *is* permitted is a stopwatch, and you see them on lots of players. But what do they do with that thing?

The short, simple answer is that they're timing rocks. There are two (two-and-a-half?) major ways that people time rocks.

The first is the "split" time. This is where you time the rock as the thrower is delivering it, usually from the near backline (or T-line) to the near hog line. This can help give the sweepers a fairly objective read on how fast the rock is going – if you've figured out that it's say 3.95 seconds from backline to hog for a draw to the button, and your thrower is coming out at 4.05, you'll probably have to start sweeping.

I say "fairly objective" and not "objective" because using split times well depends on being accurate to small fractions of a second, which is hard to do (in terms of starting and stopping the stopwatch) and takes some practice. You also have to be able to quickly determine that lower times mean faster rocks (and higher times than expected means sweep).

The time is also not strictly speaking an objective read on the speed of the rock *after release*, which is the key piece of information you're after. Rather, it's just a measure of how fast the thrower was sliding between those two points: if they dragged their knee, pushed on the rock with an arm extension at the end, or a myriad of other tweaks, the time will need a grain of salt when interpreting it.

So you have to compare to what your eyeball (or partner who is eyeballing the rock's speed) says the rock is doing, and determine whether it's your stopwatch or eye that's wrong. It's also very thrower-specific: someone who's very slippery with a long slide will time differently than someone with a slow slider who's already releasing by the near T-line. And you'll have to adjust to each thrower's release: someone who adds a bit of speed to the rock on the release will need to be interpreted differently than someone with a consistently neutral release.

In a league where you play with the same people for at least a few weeks at a time, taking split times may be more useful than a league where you're seeing a different set of slides each week.

That parenthetical "and a half" way of timing rocks comes because there are a few ways to do split times: you can use a little less space and do it from the near T-line to the near hog line, which is a shorter time and requires even more precision than backline-to-hog, but also means your thrower is cleanly into their slide by the time you're timing.

The other major way to time rocks is the hog-to-hog time, most often used by Skips watching the rocks come at them. This helps give us a sense of how fast the ice is – if a "typical" draw to the T-line is 14 seconds, and on one path it's just 13.5, that tells us the path is a little slow (which, in our backwards curling lingo, means the rock had to be thrown faster to make it through the sludgier path). It's not so helpful for calling whether to sweep a particular shot (except perhaps from the hog line to the stopping point). It can also help provide a yardstick for hits – if you call for "board weight" as a Skip, then find it's a second faster than you were expecting and also ran way straighter, well, the extra speed may be the more likely cause than that you mis-placed the broom for the line call.

When I first started looking at hog-to-hog times as a Skip, it took a full season of doing it before the numbers started making sense and being useful to me. It takes time to learn to do it consistently, and internalize what the watch is telling you about the rocks and the ice.

Playing Back End

The Role of Skip, Vice, and Experience

In our club's mixed league, people fresh out of learn to curl start at Lead. As they gain experience, they are "promoted" to Second, then Vice, and eventually, Skip.

This reinforces the (*inaccurate!*) notion that as you move through the throwing order, players should be bringing more experience to the role, and that people should want to "move up".

Ian Tetley tells the story of how after winning the Brier as a Second, a journalist asked if he'd be starting his own team as a Skip, and he replied that it would be a foolish thing to do – he was a great player at Second, and wouldn't necessarily make a great Brier-level Skip. It was a *misconception* that everyone should want to "move up the ranks."

You can be a highly experienced player who prefers front end, and conversely may be the newest one on the team but have the aptitude and desire to call the shots as Skip.

I've heard several people make the case that new players should be slotted in at Second, in part because it's really hard to build an end if the free guard zone expires and you haven't managed to get any guards in play, and in part because Seconds will get exposure to more kinds of shots (a nice mix of draws, guards, taps, hits at Second vs largely guards and draws at Lead) earlier on. Moreover, doing so helps break the unconscious thinking that there's a ranked order to the positions, and the Skip should always be the most experienced person on the team.

There is a nugget of sound wisdom there in the conventional belief: playing back end (Skip and Vice) does mean you have new variables at play, beyond what you had to deal with at Lead or Second. You start to see rocks coming toward you instead of away from you. You have to call line, decide on ice, stand as a target, and (particularly for Skips), determine the strategy. That's a lot of extra things that Leads and Seconds don't have to deal with yet, so it's nice to get some experience with "just" those aspects of the game before being thrown more.

However, there is definitely a personality/temperament factor to consider before throwing someone into the deep end of playing back end – years on the ice alone don't make a Skip.

Not everyone enjoys the strategic aspect of the game. And it can be intimidating to have to tell other people what to do, even if you happen to have the most experience. Even in casual leagues where the scores don't really matter, it can be stressful having to throw the last rock.

In some cases, even a very experienced curler may have more fun (and contribute more to a team) as Lead or Second, and a relatively inexperienced player may have more fun and contribute more at Vice or Skip.

STANDING IN THE HOUSE, HOLDING THE BROOM

The most essential function of the player standing in the house (Skip, or Vice for Skip's shots) is to set and call the line. There's strategy, too, which is used to decide the shot that is driving the line being set, but that's a different section with a lot to cover (and entire books on the topic exist). So, let's start by focusing more on the basic mechanics of setting and calling line.

Setting Line

Your broom is going to be the target for your thrower ("the line"). If you recall the steps for a good delivery, it involves setting up to your line as you step into the hack from behind, aligning your hips and everything else to the Skip's broom. That means that as Skip, you need to have your broom down and target set before your thrower gets in the hack.

But *where* do you set the broom down?

Remember the basic outline of how a shot in curling works: it's thrown to a target, with a rotation, and then **curls** to end up in the desired spot.

So first, you have to figure out what that desired outcome is – what spot should the rock stop at? That's getting into the strategy part, which we'll cover later. For now, let's assume that you have thoughtfully figured out a shot using some strategy basics... or you're going with the tried-and-true rec-level basic strategy of calling for a centre guard followed by a bunch of attempts to draw to the button.

To get a shot to finish on the centreline (or whatever your particular shot is, but we'll continue with that basic strategy of calling for a draw to the button), where do you need to put the broom down for your thrower to aim at? This is called giving the right amount of "**ice**" – "more ice" or "wider" would mean having more distance between the desired final spot for the rock and the position of the broom; "less ice" or "tighter" would mean, well, less.

This is where experience can be handy. Part of the challenge in skipping is learning the ice [*] (playing surface) and the different way your players throw to

---

[*] The terminology is a touch confusing, as ice is both the playing surface and distance given between target and outcome for curl.

figure out how much the rock is going to curl for a given shot and thus figuring out how much ice (distance between the target broom and desired outcome) to give for that shot. It's different every game, and can be wildly different from club to club. Different parts of the sheet will curl different amounts, and each of your player's releases will affect the curl, too. It changes through the course of the game! Figuring out how to account for all of these conflicting factors is part of what makes skipping challenging, but also a fun part of the game.

Having a very rough rule of thumb may be helpful, so I will provide some starting points based on our club, with a very large caveat that even here it will change game to game, and may be wildly different for your ice.

We usually get about 4' of curl, so if you want to draw to the centreline (draw or guard), you'd put the broom at about the edge of the 8' circle. After a few shots you should get a sense of how close that advice was, and adjust accordingly – if your team's rocks are not curling enough to get to the centreline, you'll need to give less ice; if they're curling past the centreline, you'll need to give more.

So you would stand with your broom on the edge of the 8', and the turn you would want would be the one that brings the rock back to the middle. The conventional way to signal for which turn to put on is to hold out one arm or the other. The rock is going to curl *from* your hand through your body out the other side, so for a shot that's going to the centre, you'd hold your arm out to the outside of the sheet (i.e., call for CW turn when standing on the right side of the line from your perspective, and CCW turn when standing on the left side of centre from your perspective).

Playing Back End

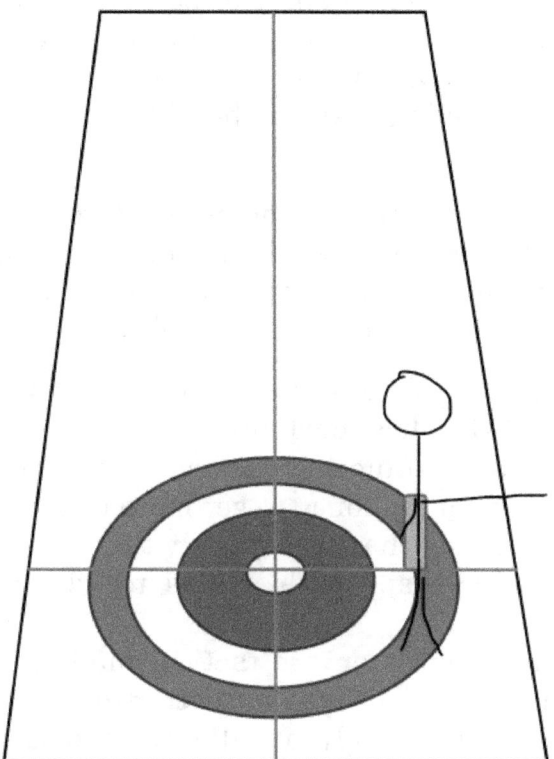

As you learn about the ice and your team's releases, you'll learn how to make adjustments to where you put the broom for a given shot.

For example, you may start on the 8' for a draw to the button call, which means you're expecting the rock to curl about 4' as it moves down the ice. After a few shots you may see that you need more or less ice, depending on whether the rocks are curling more or less than that.

You may also factor in the specific conditions and objectives of the shot: for instance, if a bunch of guards have built up, you may want to err on the side of giving more ice to be sure you get by them. If you find that the other team is deadly with their hits, you may want to err on being tight with the ice (less ice, i.e. standing closer to centre for this example shot) to be sure that your rock buries behind the guards – your sweepers can always help hold it straight but unless they've mastered directional sweeping may not be able to do much if you err on the wide side.

There will be a number of factors that go in to figuring out how much ice you need to give (i.e., how far from the desired final destination you need to put the broom to account for the expected curl), including:

- Your read of the ice: how much is that particular part of the sheet curling?
- Your understanding of your thrower: some curlers will have a tendency to get more or less curl out of their rocks than others, or they may miss the target (perhaps with a bias to which way they miss)
- Your thoughts on the tactical implications of the shot: for this set-up, is it better to call it tight and sweep aggressively, or call it wide to be sure it gets by something? Also including what the appropriate tolerances might be and what the "good misses" are
- Your thoughts on the ice needed for that specific shot: a draw will need more ice than a tap/raise, with a hit needing even less.

Similarly, to get a rock out to the edge of the 8', you could start with the broom on the centreline, or way out past the edge of the house with the other turn. In most games at my home club, I'd be tempted to take the one starting on the centreline and going out, because we usually find the edges of the sheet can be slower than the paths closer to the middle, but you may find reasons to prefer the other way.

Indeed, most shots will have two ways of pulling them off (clockwise or counter-clockwise turns), and then it's just a matter of figuring out the amount of ice for either. Sometimes in practice it can be fun to figure out the turn that feels like it's harder to call, and sometimes in the game one will feel blindingly obvious while the other feels crazy to attempt.

When figuring out how much ice you will need for a shot, remember that a hit is going to curl less than a draw or guard, but it can be more dependent on whether you're going from the centre out or the outside-in. I find hack or board-weight hits will curl 3-5' from the centre-out, but only about 1-3' from the outside-in (again, your club's ice may be wildly different). This is why many Skips prefer to take that turn when given the choice... however for some weird psychological reason (afraid of leaving the centre? not lining up properly in the hack?), many newer curlers have more trouble hitting the broom when it's further to the wings, and so you may have better luck making the harder line call from the centre-out direction.

Anyway, once you've decided on the shot and taken a guess as to how much ice you need, plant your broom, and stick a hand to the side to indicate the handle to take.

Being a Target

Before you plant that broom, you have to communicate what the shot is: a draw, guard, raise, hit? You could yell that down, but unless you have an anomalously quiet rink or loud voice, that's unlikely to be successful. Tapping your broom on the ice or another rock can help show the thrower (and sweepers) what you want the shot to be, and if needed (for a hit or raise) also give some indication of weight. See the prior section on *On-Ice Communication* for how to communicate the goals of the shot.

Then you can plant your broom to be a target.

And **plant** your broom: keep it nice and still. **You're a target**, and the last thing a thrower wants is for the target they are carefully aiming at to suddenly move just as they are nearing the release point. Indeed, stay in place *after* they let go too – it will help with calling for line, and ensure that you don't accidentally move too soon. My personal pet peeve when throwing is having a Vice or Skip take the broom away just as I'm pushing out of the hack.

Calling Line for the Sweepers

One of the first things you'll want to do after the stone is released is determine if the broom was indeed "hit" (is the shot on the right line?). That's hard to do if you've already moved the broom.

The best way to get a view to whether the shot is on line is to have your eyes also be on the line. Stand directly behind the broom on the line of delivery, which has the bonus effect of making your entire body a target. Jennifer Jones is one of the best Skips in the game in part because she was born with a broom growing directly from her belly button so she is always perfectly centred behind it (I kid, but only a little – watch some archived games and it's hard to find a shot where she wasn't carefully lined up).

Playing Back End

(Left: standing not at all in line with the broom; Right: standing nicely in line with the broom, but with the broom head flat on the ice rather than having the bright bottom side face the thrower. Ideally you should stand with the broom head up as in the left image, but with your body centred on the line of delivery as in the right one.)

Ok, so you've created the best possible target for your thrower, and in doing so put yourself in the best possible position to determine if they're on line. Whatever the result, you'll want to communicate that back to your sweepers. If the rock is inside (off the line in the direction its going to curl), then you'll likely need your sweepers to sweep to hold it straight so it won't over-curl by the end. If it's outside, you may want them to hold off on sweeping, even if it's light (depending on the shot, and depending if your team is using directional sweeping or not – if they are then you may want to call for curl). If it's on line, that's good for them to know, too.

When calling to your sweepers, you can come up with your own vernacular for when to sweep, whether or not to include directional sweeping cues, how hard to sweep, etc. But in general, I would suggest saving the "o" vowel sounds (stop, whoa, no, off) for not sweeping, and so avoid things like "go" as a sweep call.

You're now free to move your broom and yourself if you need a different view on the stone coming at you.

Standing in the house is indeed a different perspective – the other 3 players on the team are beside the rock or seeing it move down the sheet away from them. As Skip (or Vice standing in the house), you see rocks coming toward you. You'll find it's very hard to judge weight (that's the sweepers' job), but you can see the line much better than anyone else can. You can watch it evolve. You'll have to also **anticipate** the path of the stone, and get the sweepers to start sweeping **before** you're in trouble. More on that later.

Besides just standing "on the line," you have some options of where to stand as Skip. For a beginner Skip, I recommend staying on the T-line unless you need to put the broom down relative to another rock (e.g., for a raise or hit) or to be seen in front of a stone that's blocking the view. It's hard enough to visualize the paths if you're up and down and all over from shot to shot – staying at least at the same depth on the sheet will help a bit.

However, as a more experienced Skip, I'm a little more comfortable with being up and down a bit and still figuring out the paths. So I personally like to stand in front of the house if I'm calling a guard, and in the house for a draw, that way my body position helps reinforce for the thrower what the shot is supposed to be. It does make it a bit more challenging to read the paths, but I think it's worth making my job a bit harder if it helps the thrower. If you're a newbie Skip, it's probably better to keep things simpler by staying near the T-line, even when calling for guards. And if you're playing with a very experienced front-end, they probably don't need the body position reminder when throwing guards and there's no need to make things harder on yourself.

Other Duties

The back-end has a few other duties, too. When the other team is throwing, the person in charge of the house can sweep their rocks behind the T-line, or your own anywhere, *after* they are put in motion. The Vices (or whoever is in charge of the house for the last stone if you have an unconventional throwing order) determine the score for the end and do any measurements if needed.

In more competitive leagues where they track standings, typically the Vices (sometimes the Skips) have the responsibility of marking the books or reporting the end result to the scorekeeper.

THINKING IN CURVES

Curling gets its name from the curved path a rock takes down the ice, but it can be hard sometimes to internalize that fact. So much of what we do in the world gets us wired to think in straight lines and right angles. Indeed, the layout of the ice itself does us no favours: a straight centreline, with parallel sideboards, perpendicular hog and backlines.

Our first instinct when looking at a sheet of ice and thinking of the appropriate graph paper to use for curling might be something with squares/rectangles on it, like this:

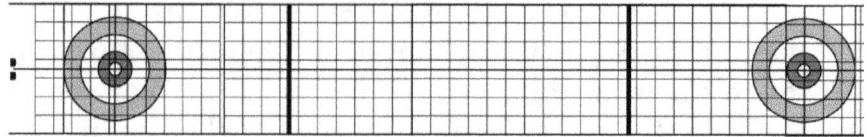

But I'd say that rectangular/square graph paper like this doesn't help for visualizing how rocks move or how we want to plot paths. Instead, we perhaps want something a little closer to this: (kind of like polar graph paper, centred on the hack)

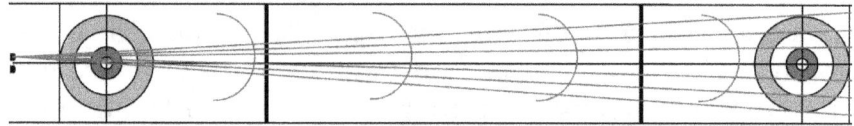

The rocks will follow curved paths down the sheet, starting off along one of those imaginary angled straight lines, and deviating more as it moves down the sheet.

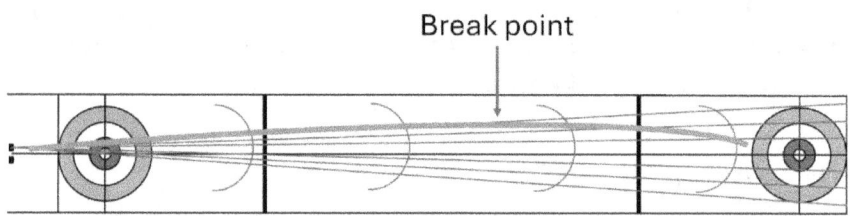

The point where you (the Skip) can tell that the path is curving and not just straight at the broom is often called the break point.

Anyway, thinking in terms of these paths can help you decide where the broom needs to go down, and when you need to call your sweepers on. You will often have to *anticipate* the curl and where the rock will go. If you're looking down the edge of a guard you need to pass by and see the thrown rock is already getting close to it, you're probably already too late to be sweeping. You will need to be sweeping earlier – back when it first started moving more quickly in that direction but still had what looked like lots of space to get by.

It's also why sometimes when a Skip wants a guard to go further to the side (in the way the images above are oriented, further *down* for the green path illustrated), they may call for sweeping. You may think that sweeping would hold it straight, but when you're well past the break point the rock is already travelling sideways. Sweeping will slow down how much *more* curl it *accumulates*, but will extend the rock further on the line it's already on, which may help get a guard to cover a certain spot. Conversely, sometimes this is why when a guard is over-curling a Skip will call you off a rock ("just let it die!"), even though in most other circumstances you sweep to hold the line.

This seems to be in conflict with the mantra "the rock goes straighter, the rock goes further" from our sweeping section. The subtle distinction to that is straighter *relative to the path it's already on*. So making the rock go further may make a guard a worse guard.

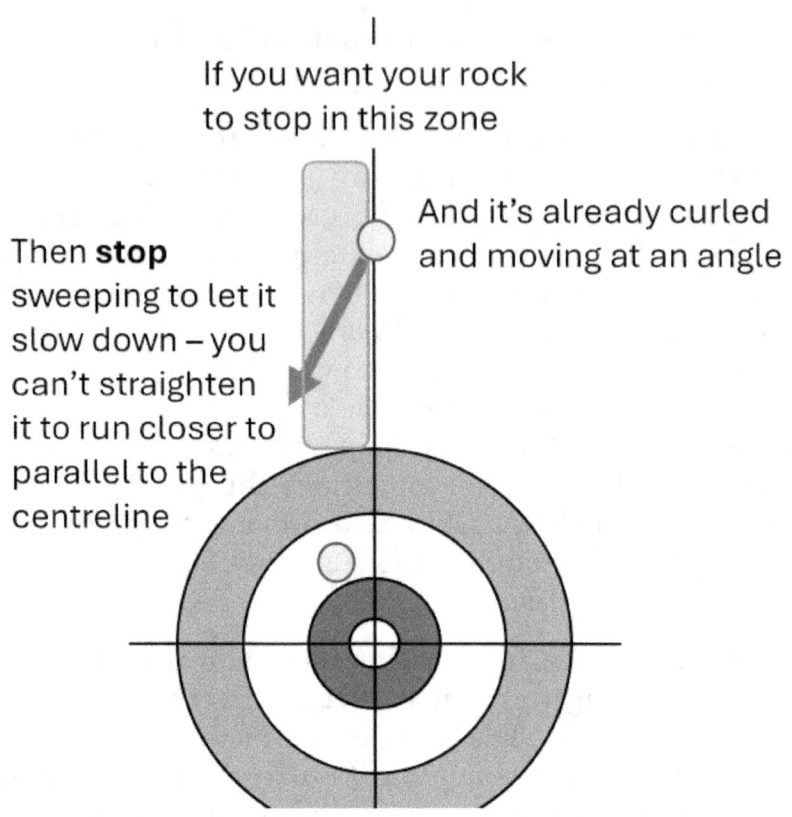

The path is dependent on a lot of things, for example different parts of the ice will yield different amounts of curl, often changing over the course of the game – mapping the ice is one of the challenges of being Skip.

Generally, higher-weight shots will run straighter than softer shots – we take less ice for a hit than a draw. A rough rule of thumb I've found helpful is to think of all paths as being basically the same shape, just stretched out by weight. So if a broom on the edge of the 8' puts a high guard on the centreline, it may be the same ice you need for the draw to come around that guard. And a hack weight shot thrown to the edge of the 8' may run by both (and hit something on the edge of the 4') but we can imagine that it would eventually get to the centreline, just out of play when it stops by the hack.

That concept also helps you remember that certain shots don't just curl a fixed distance sideways, they're following a curved path. Near the front of the house, you may need 2' of ice for a hack-weight hit, but that might just be 1' to tap a high guard, or 3' to hit a rock at the back of the house (see how the yellow trajectory that goes right to the hack curves below, and where it passes a guard, top of the house, and back of the house, relative to the guideline touching the edge of the 12', which would have been the line of delivery).

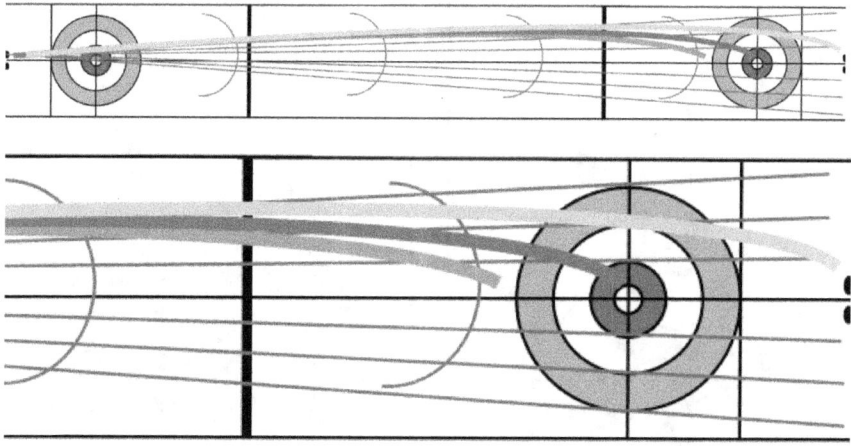

Thinking of the path a rock will take gets very important when you need to navigate a port. Sometimes the space between two guards is plenty to slip a rock through, but only with one particular turn. Since I can't animate this, I'll use multiple yellow rocks to illustrate the path the hitting rock would take.

Let's look at a situation roughly like what's shown with the blue rocks (darker for black & white viewers) – a target rock that we need to eliminate, with two guards separated by some distance, but just barely one rock width between them horizontally. It is tight, but doable... but the only way to make the shot is with the counter-clockwise turn (outside-in, left image). You can get by the first guard with an inch or two to spare and still get by the second guard because the shooter will be moving and curling *away* from the second guard and further *into the hole*.

With the other turn (right image), even if you got as close as you could to the first rock, your rock is curling *toward* the second guard, so no matter how hard and straight you throw it, you aren't getting through the port.

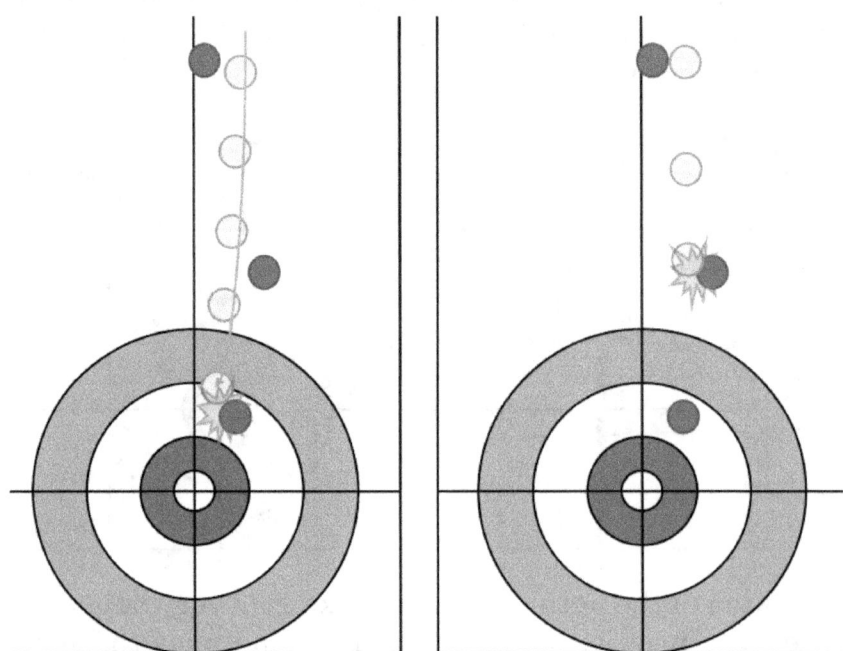

This is also important when you want to make a raise -- you have to visualize the path of the rock, and think of which path taps the rock you want to promote *partway along that path*. You will usually need less ice to make a tap than to put the rock there in the first place. Again I'll use a series of yellow rocks to illustrate the path (ignore the fact that it's a blue rock it looks like we're lining up to tap).

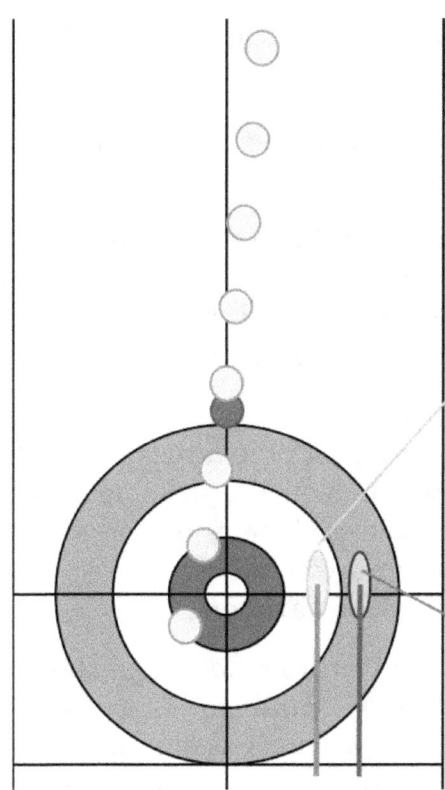

Yellow (inner): broom position to make raise (less ice than for the draw)

Blue (outer): broom position to make draw to centreline

The diagram also indicates that for a raise, you need the shooter to have more weight than where you want the raised rock to end up, but not a tonne more. Some energy/speed will be lost in the collision, but generally only 1-2 rock-width's worth for a tap directly on the nose (it depends on how "lively" the rocks are, how frozen in place the target rock is, etc.). I've heard the pros say just 1 extra rock as a rule-of-thumb but find it's a bit more than that for our rocks. So for this raise from a biter to the T-line, it only takes roughly back-button to back-4 weight.

JUDGING THE SHOT AND MAKING THE SWEEP CALL

The Skip (or Vice if they are in the house*) will be the one to watch the line and call for sweeping if needed.

As I briefly mentioned before, you have to *anticipate* the curl by thinking about the curved path the rock is on, **and you will usually find you have to call for the sweep much earlier than your first instincts might tell you.**

In most cases your sweepers will not hold a rock perfectly straight – they'll reduce how much curl it picks up, but it will still keep curling. Plus the rock may already have some lateral motion by the time you call for the sweep, though it can be really hard to see early on.

Calling for sweeping early when things look like they're getting close is also good because – and this is true but I know many of us in our first few times skipping have a hard time internalizing it – you can call the sweepers right off again. Indeed, it can feel a bit embarrassing at first to be yelling "Hard! Off! Hard! Whoa! Yep yep yep! Right off, on its own!" It feels like you're being indecisive and playing with the sweepers. But this is actually a really good thing in curling – in my opinion a perfect shot is not one that's made without being touched by the sweepers, and not one that had to be pounded end to end to make it, but one that required about a quarter effort from the sweepers – some margin for error on both sides, but a little on-off-on-off action shows just how close and perfect a shot is.

---

* Though often the Skip will *also* call line from behind after release, which may conflict with the Vice. Who gets precedence can be carefully negotiated in advance, defaulted to the person in the house, or a matter of who yells louder. The general default is the person in the house.

You will face the situation where you anticipated curl that didn't happen (possibly because of how awesome your sweepers are). You'll see your sweepers, chests heaving to catch their breath, having just over-swept a rock on your command, and if you're like me, you'll feel awful about it. It's easy to say that's a part of the game and your sweepers really will forgive you, but it's still a hard mindset to conquer.

Sorry, again that's an experience thing: try out being a Skip, get it wrong a few hundred times, and you'll start to get better. It's OK, we all had to go through it. Don't let it stop you from giving skipping a whirl!

Plus, we are none of us perfect. If you are calling the game as well as you possibly can, given random noise in the outcomes, then your team's misses should about half the time come from under-curling with some accidental sweeping, and about half the misses should be from over-curling even with some where the sweepers were standing by. There will (should!) be many shots where you accidentally called your sweepers to sweep where it wasn't needed (but more where it would have been needed and you needed to not hesitate). If you're missing too many shots with over-curl, you need to either adjust the ice you're giving (yes, that too, but that's not the part we're talking about now) or get more comfortable with putting your sweepers to work. Hey, it's good exercise.

Anyway, the trick to anticipating the curl is mapping out that curved path in your head, and judging whether the rock is currently moving as you expected, or if it's curling sooner/more than you modelled in your head (or, if using directional sweeping, less and needs a sweep for curl). This may mean calling for the sweep even though the rock is still several feet (laterally) short of the target – you have to trust and believe that the curl is going to come like you expect.

Mapping the Ice

There is a figure – you may have seen it – that I have seen three dozen times in different curling presentations, similar to the one below, showing the ice as some uneven surface, implying there may be "uphill" and "downhill" parts that affect the curl. And while that's somewhat of a useful idea, that's just not how I see the ice.

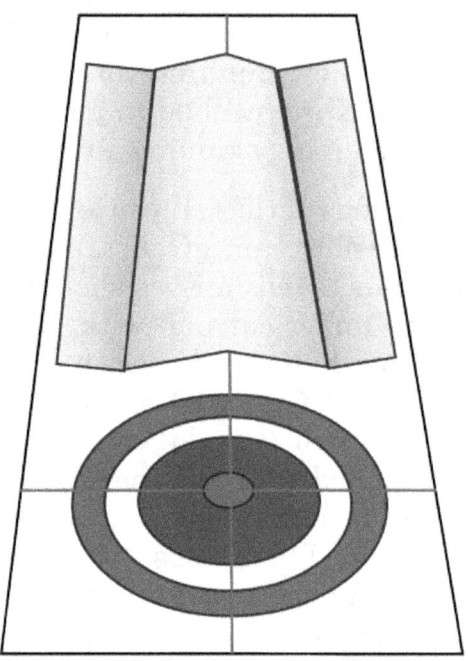

There can be ridges and runs (especially those who play on ice maintained by Zambonis* and used for skating hours before the curling game), and parts where a rock just seems to "fall", refusing to curl in one direction or even moving against the direction it should curl. There's so much more to mapping out the ice than one side vs. the

---

* Curling in a hockey arena is sometimes referred to as playing on "arena ice" by Americans, where that kind of shared space is somewhat common. "Arena ice" for Canadians more commonly refers to the ice for big competitions played in arenas, and if anything is usually *better* than dedicated club ice.

Playing Back End

other. Weird spots may be much smaller than those big sheet-length half-pipes pictured.

There are also "patches" (as I envision them) that aren't big linear runs on the ice. Areas where maybe the pebble has or has not been worn down as much as the sheet on average, or where "something undefinable but definitely funky" is happening and rocks are not curling or are suddenly breaking and cutting to the side. Certain paths and patches may run faster or slower than others, especially if there's some frost on the ice and or the pebble is fresh and unused on a path.

However you envision it, you can start to build up that map of the ice in your head – which will be different each game! – and use it to help anticipate what the rock will do and when to make your call. And that's a lot of mental work and part of what I find both challenging and fun about being a Skip... and it's perfectly fine to also handwave it away as too complicated for where you might be in your skipping journey and just always treat the ice as perfectly uniform until something clicks for you and you start to see it.

As you watch the rocks come at you, you'll slowly start building up that mental map. As a final tip, remember that you can also read the ice from your opponent's rocks. Good etiquette is to not be a distraction for the other team's throwers – stand back and out of their line of delivery while they throw (or at least very still and with your broom not as a distracting target if you are going to stand behind the other Skip). But once they've let go, you're free to move in behind the other Skip and watch the line. Where did they throw to? How is it moving? Will you need to follow them down that path next?

Plan B

A big way to improve your skipping game is by thinking about "Plan B" – what else can you get from a shot if it's different from planning in some way? If it's heavy, if it's light, if it starts curling early, if it runs straight?

This goes into shot selection (and also plays into the tolerance you can call), and hopefully at the shot selection stage you'll already start thinking about some possible alternatives so that when you see the rock coming toward you, you'll know what to do.

Regardless, very often a shot will not quite be what you called, sometimes so far different you had no way to predict it. Communication with the sweepers about what weight it actually is will help give you some notice that things are going to shift to a plan B scenario.

Then you have to adjust the sweep call to anticipate some other shot – can you get a good raise out of this? If it's too heavy, can you sweep it to rub a guard and roll somewhere useful? Working around these improvisations and thinking on the fly to change the call can be a challenging part of being Skip.

As you're making the call, it's often helpful to communicate to the sweepers that you are going for something other than the originally called shot, preferably with some kind of detail on what exactly it is you're aiming to do. Otherwise you may call for a sweep only for the front end to look up at you and go "are you sure, it's nowhere near the called path/weight?"

SCORING, MEASUREMENTS, SCOREBOARD

In addition to determining the strategy and holding the broom for the Skip's rocks, the Vice is also responsible for scoring, measuring, and putting numbers up on the scoreboard.

We covered scoring earlier – whoever is closest to the button scores! However many rocks that are touching paint that are closer than the opponent's closest get counted. It's fairly straightforward, but someone has to have the responsibility of actually counting those rocks, and that job falls to the Vices.

The Vices also have the unwritten responsibility of making sure all the other players know not to kick the rocks away until *both* Vices have agreed on the score – nothing worse than being blue and having the red team's Vice yell "two red" while you start to say "those are really close, I'll have another look..." just to have your Lead kick your rock away.

Most of the time, the score will be fairly obvious, and it will just be a matter of making sure both Vices say the score out loud (get that explicit confirmation – it's really hard to have a civil disagreement about what the score should have been if all the rocks are already cleaned up at the backboard).

Some of the time, it will be closer. Be sure to look directly down from the top of the rocks for the best view – parallax errors are very easy to make if you're standing off to the side and trying to eyeball which may be closer. However, it can easily be too close to call by eye.

For those situations, most rinks will have two measuring devices on hand, with a pinhole in the centre of the house that they are inserted into. **Note that these devices are the final word** – the rings painted on the ice may not be *exactly* round or *exactly* centred on the hole or *exactly* the right size. So although a rock may look like it's definitely on the paint, or definitely closer than another one on the other side of the rings based on how much of the paint you can see... the measuring tools may surprise you with a different reality.

The first device to aid measurements is the biter bar, a 6' rod that can spin around the rings, pivoting around the central pin. If a rock touches the biter bar, it is in, if it doesn't, it's out. The biter bar is one of the only pieces of measuring equipment that may find use before the conclusion of an end, as you may need to check if a tight guard is biting or not for the purposes of the free guard zone. If you look very closely in the picture below, you'll see that the paint is a few millimetres further out than the biter bar.

Playing Back End

The other is the measuring stick, which will have a small lever linked to a dial readout, which can move up and down the stick, then locked in place with a set screw(s). The idea is to get *close* to one of the rocks to be measured (but not right in front of/touching!), move the dial/level to where it looks like it would be in the right position to make contact with the rock, and tighten the set screws down to position it *while it is not making contact*. This is because you don't want to accidentally move the rock in the process of adjusting the measuring stick.

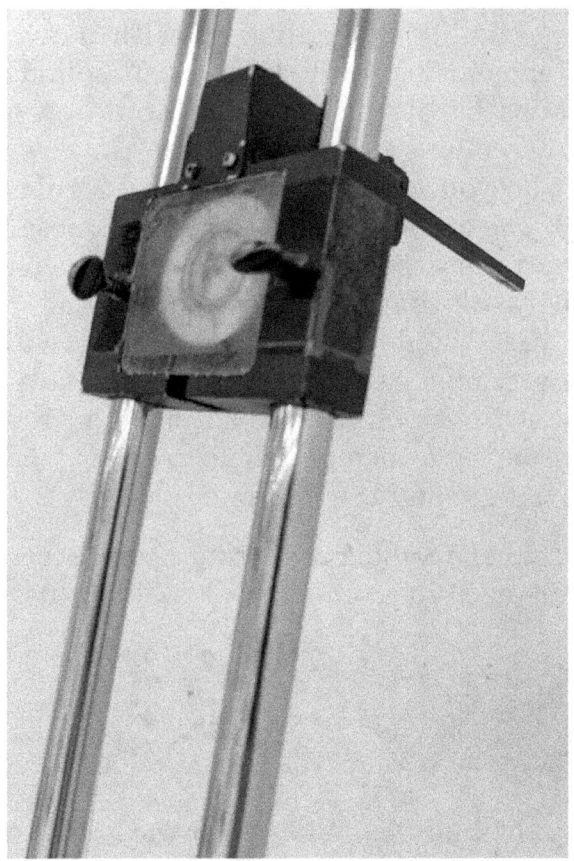

Once the dial is locked in, you can slowly swing the measuring stick around past the first rock. Make note of the maximum reading. Then continue around the house

155

to the next rock to be measured. Whichever is closer will have the higher number on the dial.

If it's so close that you want a re-measure, loosen and reposition the dial (so that you'll get different numbers) and go around again, especially if you're afraid that the dial came loose in the process for a close measure.

Good practice is to only measure in one direction (rather than going back and forth across the rocks), so go slow enough to clearly see that maximum point.

There is still the possibility of ending up with a tied measurement after measuring with the stick. It sounds incredible, as the stick can typically differentiate even small variations, to fractions of a millimeter! However rare, it may happen to you, and there are various rules for dealing with it. If one or more rocks are already closer and determined to count, then the tied rock(s) don't count. If it is the shot rock that is in question, the end is counted as a blank. Mixed doubles (again, a topic that will come in a few more sections) has a variation on the rule, so hammer usually switches on a blanked end – in the rare case of a blank coming from a tied measurement, the hammer team does not give up the hammer.

Finally, the Vices are responsible for putting up the score at the end. Many curling club scoreboards look like this:

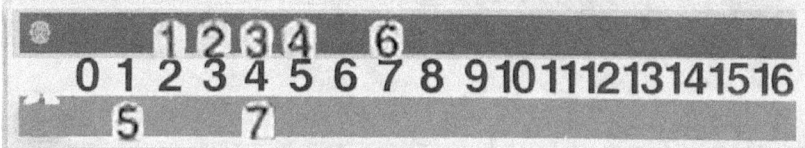

With the score down the middle, and tags for the ends. In curling, only one team can ever score in an end, so only one end tag would ever be needed. Thus this approach reduces the number of tags that need to be kept on hand. Moreover, they can be kept in order so you don't have to rummage through them to find the tag you need.

Contrast with baseball, where the ends ("innings") are across the middle, and tags are hung for the points. Multiple copies of score tags are needed to cover the possible range in scores.

Typically, the Vices would put the score up shortly after the end, when they are near the scoreboard (which may be as late as when they get to that end to hold the broom for their Skip). However, your club or league may also have some guidelines about when *not* to post the scores. For instance, at our club we generally don't put the points up once one team has more than a 5-point lead – the Vices keep score in their heads until the team that's behind scores something and then suddenly a few ends may go up at once.

STRATEGY BASICS

STRATEGY BASICS AND IGNORING THE PROS

Curling is a very strategic game. Some call it "chess on ice", except unlike chess you never know if you're going to get a rook's straight shot or a knight's hook move until you see the rock coming down the ice.

A lot has been written on curling strategy, with entire books on the subject. As this book is intended more for beginners and improvers, I will focus more on the basics of strategy.

The first basic principle is that a lot of the detailed strategy guides and what the pros do in their televised games doesn't necessarily apply to your game at the recreational level.

You have to call shots in your game *that your team actually has a decent chance of making.* A strategy guide may tell you that a hit is an easier shot with a higher probability of success, keeps an end cleaner, etc. However, if your player in the hack has a near-zero percent chance of success on a hit, it's the wrong call *for them.* Many "textbook" strategies will assume for example that the team with hammer will work toward keeping the middle free, on the assumption that the Skip can draw to the 8' at will to at least score one point. But that's not always a given at our level of play!

Strategy Basics

Conventional strategies from curling textbooks can rapidly fall apart in the hands of rookie teams. With the free guard zone, the non-hammer team can put up two guards before any hits are allowed. So to keep the middle draw path clear, someone on the hammer team has to either make some tricky tick shots or a double take-out after the free guard zone expires – far from a gimme at the recreational level. And then follow-up with an actual draw for shot with the last rock.

Likewise, the non-hammer team's strategy to steal or force (limit points) can quickly turn against them if the hammer team finds their draw weight first and simply accepts the invitation to play to the middle and uses those centre guards to put two in the 4' – the "pro" response may be for the non-hammer team to do a run-back shot with one of the guards, but that's a very low-probability shot for us mortals.

So let's start from the very basic concepts. In curling, you can score more than one point in an end, but only one team can score per end. Thus you can try to focus on:

1. Getting a point for your team

2. Getting many points for your team

3. Preventing the other team from scoring a lot

And then there are risks and trade-offs with each of those approaches: to get many points for your team, you may have to risk letting the other team score a lot.

The other basic concept to keep in mind is that games are rarely shut-outs. The other team is probably going to score at some point. Often a good strategy is, at certain points, *to let them*, and simply try to limit how many points they get when they do.

There is also the concept of the last rock advantage. You could imagine an end where the team that throws first gets a number of rocks in the house, but as long as the hammer team can put that last rock closest to the button, they will still get at least one point.

We call this a "**force**" when we make the hammer team score just a single point, and it's usually considered a minor victory even for the team not scoring – **it's the smallest price you can pay to get the hammer back**.

Indeed, you might consider an "ideal" game to be one where you score 2 points with the hammer, force the other team to 1 point, get the hammer back and score 2 points for your team, etc.

You can also score when you don't have the hammer. This is called a "**steal**".

OFFENSE AND DEFENSE IN CURLING

Offense and defense are fairly general concepts in sport. However, curling terminology does not do us any favours in making it clear what's an offensive and what's a defensive approach.

Offense, in general, is when you aim to score for your team. Thus in curling, guards and draws are considered offensive as they create more opportunities for scoring, even though "guard" is about the most defensive-sounding shot that there could possibly be.

Likewise, defensive shots are ones that reduce the odds that the opposition will score, and they can't score if their rocks are not in play. So hits are considered defensive shots in curling, even though in almost any other sport a "hit" sounds like a pretty darned offensive move.

It's weird and backwards.

Strategy Basics

One of the first steps in deciding on your team's strategy is to figure out what your natural inclination towards defensive and offensive approaches is. Are you aggressively trying to score points, and comfortable with the risk of giving up a bunch in the process? Do you prefer a closer, lower-scoring game where you manage risk and keep things a little simpler? Something in-between, where you look for opportunities but have your hand on the bail switch?

Then you have to determine what your team can make. The other reason hits are defensive is because they are supposed to be easier to execute: the shot is not quite as sensitive to the exact weight, they tend to run straight enough that giving the right amount of ice to ensure a rock goes away is a pretty high-probability call. However, if your team struggles with hits, they may not be such a defensive choice.

Keep those abilities in mind when thinking about what shot to call and your strategy: what will set up a situation where you get to throw shots that your team considers easy, and the opposing team has to throw shots that they consider hard?

PATIENCE AND IGNORING SHOT ROCK

One thing I see a lot of beginner Skips do is play almost exclusively with shot rock: *everything* is about getting to be shot, hitting the other team's rock if it's shot, or putting up a guard to protect shot.

If your style is more defensive, this may be a perfectly fine approach. If you want to be more offensive, then there may be times when you want to be more patient, and ignore shot rock to put something else up.

Particularly when shot rock is nearly on the button, it can be hard to ignore all your instincts screaming at what an awesome shot that was, *do something about it*! However, consider that it's not going to get any better from there – if you ignore it and draw somewhere else in the house, then you can see what the other team is up to, and may get some more opportunities. Perhaps they'll guard it, but imperfectly and you'll be able to hit it and sit two. Perhaps they'll hit your rock, letting you then get back to your regularly scheduled program of hitting the rock near the button and trading singles. Perhaps you'll try to draw to the top 8' and come a bit deep, tapping it back to a position where it can now help you as backing.

Remember that, especially early in the end, rocks are not necessarily in their final position: that perfect draw to the button may not be there by the time the Vices count the score, especially if a lot of little tippy-tappy shots into the middle get made. If you like the way the way an end is shaping up, you don't immediately have to go chasing shot rock.

Even though it's further from the button, early in an end a rock in the top 12' may be much more threatening because it can help control the middle: blocking draws in, being something that can be raised up later.

This brings us to one bit of conventional strategy that's helpful to consider even at the earliest stages of learning to Skip: the control zone.

Strategy Basics

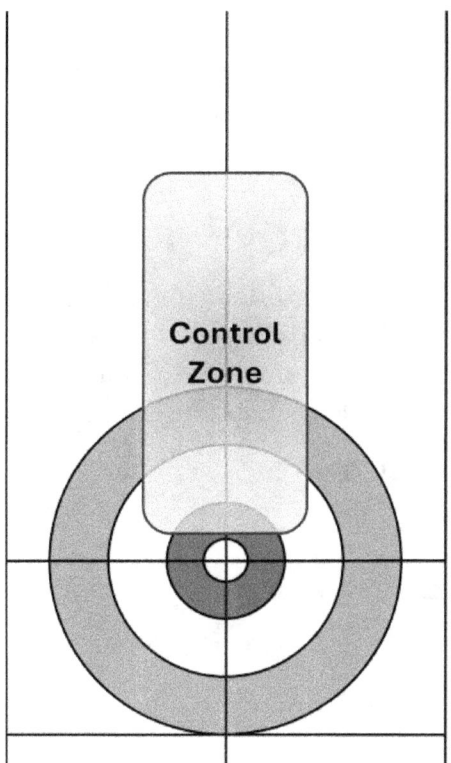

Rocks close to the house or at the top of it can help you control what happens at the button. Early in the end, if you want to play offensively, you may want to focus more on getting rocks there than necessarily going straight for the 4' ring or button.

Try to set up positions where your team can score, or keep the other team from scoring a bunch. Think about rocks in the control zone (for your team, especially without hammer), and keeping the other team out of there (especially when your team has the hammer).

And for basic strategy, think about those very simple possible results from an end: how can you make it so that your team scores, or you keep their team from scoring a lot? When is the right time to try to take some risks to score more, when do you want to just get granite out of play to keep it simple? How can you try to set up this shot (and the next?) so that you are throwing something with lots of margin of error, and they'll have to throw something for the highlight reel?

FrESHAIR

Conventional strategy guides (including the NCCP coach training) "simplify" curling strategy down to *seven* factors, which to me seems like a lot to throw at people just learning to be Skip. They do form a cutesy acronym:

- **F**ree Guard Zone
- **E**nd
- **S**core
- **H**ammer
- **A**bility
- **I**ce
- **R**ocks left to throw

For FrESHAIR.

You can see how each of those will be important: the free guard zone is critical at high levels of play, where without it defensive-minded teams would just peel everything (and the fact that they were doing just that is what led to its invention in the first place).

You may take fewer risks if you're already up on the scoreboard, and more if you're desperate to come back from behind. Particularly as you get closer to the end of the game.

Whether or not you have hammer will change your strategy – conventional wisdom is to try to set your team up to score two or more with hammer, which often involves playing to the wings early, and trying to keep the middle open for a draw with last rock. While without hammer you may try to bring play to the middle to either steal or force.

It can be hard to juggle all of those factors as a relatively new Skip.

Plus, the relative importance of some of those factors to the pros doesn't necessarily apply for new/very recreational players. For example, in our competitive leagues if we want to set up to steal, we may call for a guard to only be about halfway between the hog line and the house to ensure that it doesn't touch the paint. Because if it is on the paint and thus not protected by the free guard zone, the other team may immediately hit it. That "Fr" factor from FrESHAIR. However, in our leagues with new players, I call for a tight guard or to come right into the house: the odds of the opposing team's Lead successfully making that hit are relatively low – I don't really need the protection of the free guard zone at all.

Tactics

There is a difference between *tactics* and *strategy*: strategy may be your plan for the end before you even get into it, the basic roadmap and principles for your shots. The tactics are picking the specific shot to call.

Here, matching tactics to player preferences and abilities is more critical. Your strategy, for example, may dictate that you should call a hit at a certain point in a game.

However, even with that strategic guidance, you have many tactical options to accomplish it. You can throw clockwise or counter-clockwise approaches, a fairly light-weight hack shot, or a peel that's set to blast through the back wall and end up outside in the parking lot.

Thinking about what you know about the paths on the ice, your player's ability and preferences, and the alternatives that each choice offers are going to be critical to your specific shot selection.

Indeed, thinking back to our discussion of "tolerance" earlier on, consider what the tolerance for the shot is. What is the "pro miss" going to look like, where you can still get an acceptable outcome from the shot? For example, early in an end trying for a draw is good, but a guard is also just fine. For one hit you may want to play down-weight, as keeping the shooter and merely bumping the target to the back 12' may be fine, while for another you may want to call for up-weight shots because you want any little tick on a guard to move that sucker far out of the way. Trying to get your strategy and shot selection to a point where your team can throw shots with lots of ways to have good outcomes is probably going to help you more than one that requires perfect execution.

But you have to balance your tactical choices with the realities of what your players are able to deliver for you – what is *their* tolerance? In some leagues, throwing anything from hack through to a normal weight hit may be an everyday affair, while in others your choices for hits may be "hack with clockwise turn" and "hack with counter-clockwise turn."

Trying to think a shot or two ahead is where your tactics and strategies will cross paths.

Three guiding questions that can help focus your mind on preparing the options for your next shot as the other team is throwing are:

1. If they miss this shot, what would I throw?
2. If they make this shot, what would I throw?
3. If I were them, what would I want to see?

That way if they do make or wildly miss their shot, your broom can go down right away, keeping the pace of play up.

And think about those very basic options: how can you make it so that your team scores, or you keep their team from scoring a lot? When do you want a complicated, tippy-tappy type end, and when do you want to just get granite out of play to keep it simple? How can you try to set up this shot (and the next?) so that you are throwing something with lots of margin of error, and they'll have to throw something for the highlight reel?

SHOT SELECTION AND THE SPOOKY CENTRELINE

There are several contradictory ideas that I hold in my head at the same time about curling ice and the physics of a shot.

1. Curling ice is a plane the rocks travel on and the little lines painted underneath it are pretty meaningless to the physics. The edge of the sheet is no harder to slide towards and hit than the centre, and shouldn't influence which shot I want to give my shooter (assuming I am the Skip here). The rocks follow the rules of physics and move in ways that are, in principle, predictable.
2. The ice **should be** a nice, uniform playing surface, **but is not**. I have to adapt to what I think I know about each part (e.g., is it frosty out there, running straight over here?) in picking a shot and determining how much ice to give.
3. The centreline is full of ghosts that like to do weird things to rocks.

Or, perhaps with a more physics-based explanation, I suspect the centreline is where the two passes of the nipper* cross (or possibly *don't cross* and leave a ridge of un-touched spiky pebble) and rocks curl weird across it.

So if I am intending to call a hit on a rock, on a textbook perfect sheet of ice it should not matter which turn I decide to call: the ice should behave more-or-less the same regardless. If I'm calling for a shot that is fast enough that it basically runs bullet-straight (say "normal" in a common vernacular of hit weights, or a 9-second hog-to-hog time: two levels more than board), it *really* should not matter which turn I take. But I will always try to avoid the one that takes my rock across the centreline.

For it is haunted.

Taking different turns for
a hit on the blue rock

Broom for CCW turn, "inside-out"

Broom for CW turn, "outside-in"

---

* A piece of icemaking equipment with a sharp, raised blade that *nips* (cuts) the top of the pebble; used to prepare a sheet for play.

So most of the time, with no guards to constrain which turn I'm going to choose, I'm going to try to take the outside-in turn for a hit.

I find generally, at our club, the inside-out shot will curl more than the outside-in one, so I'll have to start by giving more ice, maybe 2-3 rock widths' worth versus maybe not even a full rock's worth of ice coming the other way (your club's conditions may vary). If I'm wrong on how weight-sensitive the curl is and it actually runs straight (or hugs the centreline *because of ghosts*), the shot will be missed because the broom is starting more than a rock-width away from the target. Whereas with the outside-in, I'm assuming we'll get maybe ~1 rock of curl. If the broom is a little less than a rock width out and we get that rock of curl, we should hit just a little inside of the nose. If it curls a bit more, we still get a piece on the side closer to centre. Even if it runs arrow-straight we should still pick it from the high side.

One thing I've struggled with finding a good way to explain (even to myself) is *why* those hits that go from centreline-out seem to be so much more release-sensitive than the ones that come from the outside-in, and why they tend to curl more in the first place.

And that's just the consideration of what the ice might do normally, with a well-thrown rock. I find that the inside-out call here is *much* more sensitive to the player's release. In particular, if the rock gets started even a little it will be *gone*. (That is, if the player nudges the rock in the direction it's to go as they add the handle, for whatever reason if they do that from the centre heading out, the rock just takes off, while you may still be able to hold it with sweepers if it's coming from the outside and nudged in just a bit).

However, there can be times when I'd try the other way. A big one is if a player is, for whatever reason, having trouble hitting the broom when the broom is placed out wide. It's somewhat common in newer players: so often our practice slides are made down the centreline that it can seem weird to line up to the edges (or, worse, a player may not line up to the broom at all, and only makes draws and guards by sliding narrow and pushing the rock out, but those shots are sufficiently insensitive to actually hitting the line that they don't notice the errors).

Another big one is if that's the only path available because of guards in the way.

A factor that's maybe not hugely important for most of our shots but **can** be another factor in the choice is the **gear effect**. If you wanted to hit the rock in the above diagram on the side closer to centre and roll to the other side of the house (perhaps to make a double on another rock not shown or get behind a guard), the gear effect will have the momentum from the spin adding to that roll for the inside-out turn, and not from the outside-in – the roll will be "livelier" for that choice.

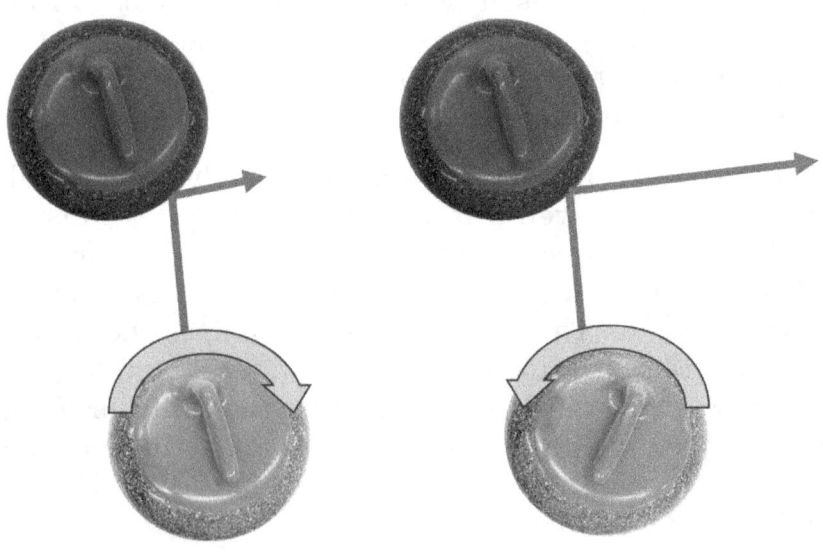

You can demonstrate the gear effect to yourself with very soft shots: in practice throw just a few feet into a rock to get a collision, with fairly fast rotation. The one with the rotation *into* the target rock will have a "lively" bounce off, while the one with the rotation *away* from the target rock will have a "dead" bounce.

A rotation "into" a target can be another bit of confusing curling terminology: after all, the rotation may take one part of the rock away from the target while bringing another in. So imagine those arrows across the top of the thrown rock: do they point into the target or away? That does mean the same rotation will be "into" or "away" depending on which side of the target you're hitting: a clockwise rotation will be "into" the target when hitting the left side of the target's centre, and "away" from the target when hitting the right side (as viewed from the direction the thrown rock is travelling, as these diagrams are set up).

POTPOURRI

I never fully understood how "potpourri" came to mean "miscellaneous" – I always envision it as a rather *specific* thing, a bowl of fragrant plant material used to perfume things.

However, an instructor in an editing seminar I had once said that the presence of a "miscellaneous" section indicates that you have not sufficiently structured your book and need to edit it again, so I desperately search for synonyms to say that I have not resorted to a miscellaneous section at the end.

Indeed, this is *clearly* a collection of dried plant matter meant to improve the fragrance of the book as you approach the end of our time together.

EQUIPMENT

Curling is a fairly equipment-light sport, especially compared to hockey or skiing. The core pieces of kit you would want to get for yourself would be shoes and a broom, warm clothes, plus a few other optional accessories.

Shoes

At the most basic level, any clean pair of shoes used exclusively for curling will work: you can throw on some grippers and get a slip-on/step-on slider. If you're new to sport and not yet ready to invest in purpose-built shoes, consider that if you're going to get a pair of running shoes *at some point* anyway, you may as well use them for curling for the first few months, and then it's basically zero incremental cost for the sport.

However, a set of purpose-built shoes will be a good investment if you stay with the sport, partly for convenience, but mostly because you can slide faster (i.e., have less friction) with them.

For the most part, to pick the right pair for you the differentiating qualities will be normal shoe things: how comfortable are they, how warm are they, how heavy are they, what materials are they made out of? The parts unique to curling (the slider, the gripper) will have some options on top of that, but those are very competitive between brands and likely won't drive your choice of shoes.

The slider on almost all recent shoes will come in two parts, allowing you to bend your shoe in the middle. Many are user-selectable (which means you often have to pay more for it above the sticker price of the shoes). The main difference will be the speed: thicker Teflon (1/4") will be faster than thinner (5/32" or 1/8").

Faster sliders are generally good, but they are less forgiving: if your foot is not directly under your centre of mass, it will just keep sliding out. Various guides are torn on which to pick: some suggest beginners start with a slower (thinner) slider, others say to go straight to a 1/4". I say it depends on what you want out of the sport and your equipment: if you want to be able to slide faster and make those big-weight takeout shots, and are willing to put up with a steeper learning curve, go right to a 1/4" (fast) slider. If you want to ease your way into the sport and don't mind having to upgrade your shoes in a second step later (perhaps a few years later when they may be wearing out anyway), then go with a slower slider to start. For modular shoes, you may be able to upgrade the slider later (though those are still like $60) without having to replace the entire shoe.

Grippers

Whether you are wearing two grippers over running shoes, or just one over a slider for dedicated shoes, you will need grippers in this sport. Grippers are a **wear item**: they're good for roughly one year per day of the week played. After that, you'll notice the fingerprint-like treads starting to wear out, which can affect how well they grip this ice. However, long before the grip is seriously degraded, the rubber material will start to flake, polluting the ice with tiny black flecks.

So plan to replace it periodically. However, an important note: grippers may come coated in a slippery mold release agent. **Wash and allow to dry before using your gripper for the first time.** (You don't necessarily have to take it home for that – in a pinch you can wash it in the washroom at the club with hand soap, just let it dry well before wearing it)

Clothes

For the most part, any old sweater or jacket will do to keep your top warm. Just remember layers – particularly when sweeping, you may get too warm and have to peel some off.

For gloves, you'll want something warm enough for you, but also with good grip on the broom. Dedicated curling gloves often have a leather palm or silicone treatments to help provide a good grip. Similar to grippers, sometimes those grippy surfaces on the palms of gloves can start to fall apart with age: if yours are peeling and flaking, it's time for a new pair (though they'll typically last more than one season).

Be careful of wool or cotton gloves/mittens, they may not have enough grip for sweeping.

Potpourri

For pants, stretch is going to be a **big** factor, to enable the slide. For many years I used some moderately stretchy golf slacks, which I would also wear around on non-curling days. They were cheaper than dedicated curling pants but stretchier than jeans and I thought I had made a wise decision... until one day I ripped the crotch wide open on a delivery. Since then, I've stuck to pants specifically make for curling, which are significantly stretchier than the off-the-shelf pants with 'some' stretch.

Each manufacturer will often have pants in different weights, including some nice warm ones with a fleece lining for Skips or those who get chilly, and others that are thinner and cooler.

Yoga pants are also a great option, and you may see several people rock them around your club.

Brooms

For brooms, lighter is going to be better. It's much easier to get the broom going back and forth when it has less mass to move. While everyone's budgetary restrictions are a bit different, generally the price difference from fibreglass to carbon fibre is not that steep, so you should just jump right to carbon fibre when you're ready to buy your own broom.

Feel free to ask another curler to try their broom to see if you like the shape of it: Hardlines taper down toward the head (they get skinnier), which makes it a bit harder to grip, but supposedly helps increase stroke speed with the change in weight distribution. Goldlines are straight right through, and BalancePlus' latest gets wider toward the head[*].

---

[*] With fairly rapid innovation and changes in equipment, we will have to see how well this section ages. Take with a grain of salt and shop around, dear curler of the future.

Up until a few years ago, many heads were a complete package and had to be replaced whole, with screws and a unique shape for each type of broom. Hardline was kind of revolutionary in that you only had to replace the fabric outer coating, making replacements cheaper. On top of that, their fabric was tough and washable, so you could wash it a few times before needing to replace it outright. Goldline (Impact) and BalancePlus (LiteSpeed RS) now use a similar approach.

That fabric generally comes in two flavours: a version for recreational play (that's us!)* that's more durable and lasts longer than the WCF-approved fabric†. Without getting into a long diversion, the WCF-approved fabric was designed to be less effective at directional sweeping and to consistently put teams on an even footing. Longevity and cost were *not* design considerations, so at the club level you should not be using that fabric (I mean, you're welcome to if you want to, you'll just be replacing your broom head five or ten times as often as the rest of us while paying more for each head).

Some brooms come with stiffening plates (i.e., a thin piece of plastic) that go between the foam and the fabric. The general consensus across many clubs is that even at the rec level, those are beyond the pale and you shouldn't be using them for good sportsmanship (but there often isn't an explicit rule banning them so you won't get in trouble if you just don't know better yet – though be sure to check your specific club's directives or take the temperature of fellow curlers in your leagues).

Delivery Sticks

If you want to deliver with a stick, there are several styles of delivery stick you can purchase. A dedicated device

---

* Confusingly called the "pro" head by Hardline.
† "Maxim" at Hardline, "eLite" at BalancePlus, "pro" at Goldline.

with a fibreglass (or carbon fibre) shaft similar to a broom, with an articulated head on end that will attach to the rock is a common option. You may be able to buy the head separately and order a broom shaft from your favourite curling supplier and attach it in lieu of a broom head.

Another option is a combination broom and delivery stick. They come in two varieties, where the slot for attaching to a rock handle is on the same end of the broom as the broom head, or when they are on opposite ends of the shaft. These have the advantage of only needing one piece of equipment to haul around, but have the minor downside of either obscuring your view of the attachment to the rock by having the broom head in the way, or of having a broom head up by your hands when the other end is busy delivering a stone.

Telescoping shafts are also available. I'm personally a little skeptical on the value of those, as it provides a joint that may collapse or spin mid-delivery if not properly locked in place. The advantage is that you can adjust the length and transport them more easily.

Particularly for people who are using a delivery stick because of mobility issues, getting *two* may be a good idea: being able to leave one at each end may save having to make an extra trip each end to make sure the stick is in the right place when your turn to throw comes up.

Other Accessories

Stopwatches: Some stopwatches are specifically designed to go on your broom if you prefer to have them there, and others you can wear on a rope around your neck or waist, or just throw them in your pocket. No complex science here, they're stopwatches. Indeed, anything more complicated than times and splits may not be permitted equipment.

Stabilizers: These balance aids can provide a wider, sturdier base to support your delivery. If you are finding it hard to deliver with a broom as your aid, try a stabilizer – your club may have one you can borrow to try. The main downside of a stabilizer is that it's an extra piece of equipment to keep track of and lug around. If you want one of your own, there are a variety of styles to choose from different manufacturers.

Compression sleeves: You may see a few sweepers wearing different devices to apply pressure for different reasons. Knee sleeves and tennis elbow bands may be to help keep certain tendons from hurting. But some people also wear a compression sleeve up their whole arm. These are instead for performance purposes. The compression is supposed to help your muscles recover from a bout of sweeping faster, to be ready for the next rock. They can also help reduce soreness after a whole game of sweeping. I personally use one when playing front end or doubles, and find that it helps, but can't completely tell you it's not just a placebo.

Solo cups: The brand name isn't critical, but people generally recognize the kind of plastic cup I'm referring to when I say a Solo cup – something very light that will bounce away easily if, say, it's used as a target for a rock in practice and gets hit. Small pylons also work well, but drinking cups can be even lighter, which can help when playing "kick the cup" when trying to slide to a specific point in practice.

Laser level: As a practice tool, laser levels can be handy for really visualizing the line of delivery (and providing a line you can actually follow in practice). You may need to find one that *doesn't* auto-level itself so that you can point the line in the direction you want.

Video camera: It can be way easier to spot and review an issue with your form if you can record yourself throwing or sweeping. So, a video camera and review system (along with a friend or coach to do the recording) can be a handy practice aid. Fortunately, these days many of us have a high-definition video camera with built-in playback capabilities in our pockets at all times.

Head Protection

Concussions are no joke, and we play on ice, which is slippery and hard, so accidents can and do happen.

Unfortunately, we're not allowed to say that various head protection solutions will save you from a concussion – there have been no controlled studies testing that, and medical claims like that require lots of evidence. So that stymies people from broadly recommending helmets or headbands. Nonetheless, common sense suggests that having *something* to cushion a fall against hard ice is going to be better than *nothing* (Not. Medical. Advice!) and is maybe not the worst idea. A full-on helmet is going to be the best choice for protection, with full coverage of your head and a chinstrap to make sure it doesn't go anywhere in a fall. Hockey helmets are one option, and several companies make curling helmets now. Bike helmets are also an option.

I personally have settled on a few different headbands as a compromise – not quite as much protection as a helmet, but less bulky. The Dynasty ones feature a new-fangled material that is gel-like most of the time, but hardens on impact (which, in part, is a way to absorb the impact's energy through a phase shift). It goes all the way around my head (but not the top). The Ice Halo is high density foam, similar to what lines a hockey helmet (just without the hard outer shell). I also own one from Crasche that has a set of inserts with a hard polycarbonate plastic outer shell and a thin lining of neoprene. I don't personally have a Goldline one, but they are fairly popular at our club and you may have seen people with them – they have a harder foam similar to what a bike helmet has, in a pad just at the back of the head.

Many other styles are available too, such as ball hats and toques to look a little less like head protection, but still with some kind of padding (often just at the back in those styles).

For all of these options, because there is no chinstrap they should fit **snug** – tight enough that if your head goes whipping around in a fall they stay in place.

Aside: *hey John, why do you have so many when you only have one head?* Partly because I thought it was an important topic and wanted to review them head-to-head*, and then wanted to be able to show people what the options were when many can only be ordered online sight-unseen. Partly because they do get sweaty and damp if you're out there sweeping a lot in a game, and if you have multiple games in day you're going to want to switch to a different one.

THE PERFORMANCE DIP

Learning a new physical skill, like sliding for the curling delivery or the footwork for sweeping, goes through several stages in your brain.

When you are first learning it, everything is new and hard. In your brain, your motor cortex and other areas of your higher-level processing centres are determining the movements. It's almost like your brain saying "ok, quad, you have to pull the knee up like this, good, now hamstring on the other leg, you have to contract like this

---

* You can read my blog post on some styles here: http://www.holypotato.net/?p=2120

and push against that rubber bit together with the gastrocnemius..." it is computationally expensive, slow, hard, and awkward. As you repeat it and practice it, the pattern of movements gets programed into your cerebellum, your thoughts are more streamlined and all of that higher-level processing simplifies to "hey cerebellum, tell the legs to 'kick into the slide phase.'"

While it's always nice to learn it perfectly correctly the first time, it can be really tough to do that and make corrections when you're barely keeping your feet under you. Instead, you may need to go through your initial learn-to-curl phase, get some games and/or practice time under your belt, and then come back around to another round of refinement and learning once you're fairly comfortable with the basics.

And then, as you do make changes, odds are good that you will find you have a "performance dip." You may be missing more shots even though your form in your slide is better. At this point it can be very tempting to revert to your old habits.

Part of why this happens is that it takes time for the change to integrate with everything else, such as your feel for draw weight. It can also be that the change is forcing your cerebellum to rewire that automatic programming, so you have to use the more computationally expensive and klutzy parts of the brain to accomplish the task – like you were a beginner all over again.

For example, perhaps you learned to slide with your broom almost straight out to your side. It seemed intuitive to help hold you up – maximum tripod spread that way for maximum stability! However, it was pulling your shoulder out, which made it harder to stay on line. Your coach noticed and helped correct your broom position, but now you have to get used to the balance in the new position all over again. And your body keeps automatically reverting every time you get in the hack, and so instead of focusing purely on what you want the shot to accomplish, you have to keep reminding yourself of where to plant your broom. So even though your shoulders line up better, you're feeling a little wobbly and missing shots for a while. This is the performance dip in action.

Fortunately, in this very real and personal example, I did eventually get used to sliding with my new broom position, and did start hitting the broom a little more consistently than before. And it did eventually become more automatic. But the performance dip was very real, and it was tempting to abandon it for "real games," which probably would have just slowed my progress down more unless I wanted to book two weeks' worth of practice ice.

PRACTICE

Having an extra night of curling certainly helps get some more repetitions in, see some more scenarios, and try more shots. And my general motto *is* more curling is much better than less curling.

However, if you want to actually work on a particular issue or change something up in your delivery, nothing beats a focused practice session where you can work on that one area. A half-hour block of practice ice doesn't *sound* like a lot compared to a two-hour game, but when you're the only one throwing rocks, you can a lot of granite moving. Indeed, you can easily get more repetitions in in 30 minutes than you can in a game, not to mention the ability to try specific things you need to work on.

Potpourri

Getting better and improving at the sport will definitely happen faster if you include dedicated, focused practice in your routine. And not necessarily just for trying fancy things or working out particular issues: **nailing the fundamentals and owning the basic positions are key elements of being a good curler**. Including practices focused specifically on the basics is important to driving that continual improvement.

Especially if there is something in particular that you want to work on, you may need some practice time to get that focus – you never know what shot you may get called to make in a game, and then you'll be distracted by the game outcome rather than working on your process.

There are lots of great lists of various drills to try online. Indeed, far too many for most recreational curlers to get through when we typically only have a few practice ice slots each season.

A few of my favourites include something for **balance**, such as sliding with no rock, then no broom. Trying to slide to specific points on the ice with no rock. Something for **line**, such as sliding to a plastic up, between two rocks or pylons, or using a laser level to create a line to slide (and deliver) along on the ice. Something for **weight control**, like trying to throw one rock anywhere, then put 4 more frozen or at least within a broom handle of it, or progressing forward or back a small increment, like throwing your first rock to the back house, and trying to throw each successive rock a little shorter while fitting them all between the backline and hog line. And something for specific shots, such as getting a friend (to make sure rocks don't fly off to other sheets or damage the hacks) to help set up shots for throwing take-outs. And don't neglect **sweeping**: as long as you have that friend with you, let them throw some shots while you try to sweep them to specific places (e.g., try to make team shots to the button, practice directional sweeping to see if you can do it and how much you can make a rock curl vs. when you sweep to keep it straight).

There are a lot of resources for practice drills out there, including entire books just full of practice drills.

There are several online resources for drills, including Curling Canada https://www.curling.ca/coaching-information/curling-drills/

Matt Bean's Curling Class YouTube channel has several drills (search for "curling drills" to find them faster, he does have them well-titled): https://www.youtube.com/@CurlingClass/

One of the resources on the Curl Coach site is a book of 40 curling drills https://www.curlcoach.com/Curl_Coach/resources.html

Finding a Coach

Individual practice is great, and may or may not be all you want from the sport. And while we do (in my not-so-humble opinion) a great job at Unionville in our learn-to-curl program, there's only so much we can do in 8 hours over 4 weeks. Your learn-to-curl was likely similar: you picked up the basics, got good enough to be placed into a game scenario, and then it's up to you if you want to put in the work to get any better.

Plus there's so much new stuff being thrown at you in a sport as complex and subtle as curling that it's hard to pick it all up perfectly. Circling back after a few months/years of playing and you're no longer fighting the basics can help you refine those skills and get to the next level.

A coach – whether in an individual setting or group clinic – can really help accelerate your progress, by identifying and correcting various issues you may have, helping to adapt the delivery to the needs of your body, or answering other questions you may have. Many clubs have coaches you can contact, usually by contacting your club's manager you can find out the process for hiring one.

Our club also conducts clinics at various points in the year, where in small groups there may be specific skills being worked on, such as delivery analysis or strategy discussions. I would guess that your club has similar options. In particular, look out for the announcement about clinics at the start of the season, as that tends to be a common time to run some tune-up sessions (and at least at our club, those ones tend to fill up very quickly, so you need to be quick on the uptake when the announcement comes out).

And it may be a little over the top to even suggest, but there are also curling camps you can attend if you're interested (and can afford what is basically a minivacation). Hot Shots (https://hotshotscurling.com/) runs a camp in Ontario (usually Oakville) and also at a few places around the world. It's like an intensive learn-to-curl, where you have more time to dive into all the topics, cover more advanced material than we can get into in our learn-to-curl (like strategy, drag and gear effects, different sweeping positions, etc.), and have some top-level coaches help correct any issues you may have. There's a similar camp out of British Columbia (Four Foot https://www.kelownacurling.com/spiels/fourfoot/), and the US and other countries likely have their own versions of these intensive camps.

Whether you pick one of those options or just get an untrained buddy to hit the practice ice with you, having an external observer look at what you're doing and give you feedback can help you improve much better than throwing rocks in practice and trying to guess what the issue might be and self-diagnose.

WARMING UP BODIES, COOLING DOWN SLIDERS

Before going out to play, it's important to do a little warm-up.

Generally, a warm-up should include something to get the heart rate up and the cardiovascular system ready to work. Jumping jacks, a light jog, or constantly forgetting your stopwatch and then your gloves and somehow your broom too in the locker room and doing a few laps of the stairs all work.

You'll also want to ensure that the muscles and connective tissues that are going to be working get warm. That's your arms and shoulders for sweeping: big windmill movements work well there. For throwing, your legs and hips: high steps, lunges, split squats work well to get those ready to go.

Your equipment may also need a warm-up, or rather, a cool down: your sliders may retain a fair bit of heat from the lounge or your locker, and be warm when you first hit the ice. It's generally a good idea to swirl them around in an unused part of the ice before taking your practice slide, to reduce the amount of melting down the pebble that will happen in the slide path. It will also help prevent your slider from being overly slippery on that first push when it's extra warm and melting pebble under it.

After the game, stretching is a good tip to help ease into recovery.

OFF-SEASON TRAINING

We've built up a lot of weird, specific flexibility throwing rocks all winter long. You don't want to lose that and get all stiff and sore the first few games back next fall. So your first prescription is to **stretch in the off-season**: get down in the delivery position and hold it for a few seconds. Do it at least a few times a week to help maintain that flexibility in your hips that's hard to come by any other way. October is going to suck a whole lot less if you keep that up.

Maintaining your fitness in other ways is also going to be important. If you're like me and have trouble self-starting for workouts but make it out to play in a league, then consider joining a summer sport of some kind for that weekly commitment. If you're more self-starting with workouts, then there are some out there to help you build the strength and fitness to be a better curler.

An excellent resource is Stephanie Thompson and her business, Empowered Performance (https://empoweredperformance.ca/), which focuses on exactly that. In addition to her paid services and programs, she has a newsletter, podcast, and lots of articles on her site to help you out.

For strength in throwing and to avoid injury, building strength and flexibility in your legs, hips, and lower back is going to help a lot. Conveniently, building strength there is also really important for aging well and not making that "uuurrrrrrgghh" noise every time you get out of a chair. Improving your balance will also help you avoid falls, which are a major factor in maintaining health as you get older.

For sweeping, upper body and core strength will help you get more pressure on the broom to be more effective, and cardio workouts will help you recover from each bout of sweeping and keep going longer for each rock you have to carry. Again, you can look to Empowered Performance for specific workout programs, but the usual suspects of moving weights, doing push-ups, core workouts like mountain climbers and planks are going to help.

The most important message if you want to stop reading here is just do *something* over the summer break, and try to keep that mobility up for curling's weird positions and movements. I can share a few tiny personal anecdotes on that importance.

First off is the difference getting those stretches in makes at the beginning of the season. For *so* many years I would not get into the curling delivery position outside of the curling season. Finally, a few years ago it clicked in my head (because, let's face it, Stephanie said so) that I could be a better curler if I put even the tiniest bit of effort in during the off-season. So I started to stretch, just ~2-3 reps of ~10-15 seconds of getting into the curling position on my way to bed at night in the off-season. Then that fall, instead of spending the first three weeks of the season stiff and sore as my body re-learned how to stretch and slide, I was good to go right from the start.

It doesn't take much. *Some effort is better than zero effort.*

Second is sweeping training. I pretty much exclusively played Skip for quite a number of years, so when I started mixed doubles I realized I had a lot of work to do on my sweeping game. Fortunately, my family is filled with seriously deranged hoarders* so we still had an Aerobi-Slide from the 80's. In the summers I would set it out on the floor, grab my broom, and pull up an archived game from the Scotties or Brier – Curling Canada's streaming platform (https://plus.curling.ca/) has a tonne of options

---

* It's a legitimate problem, please send help.

in their archive, and I never manage to catch more than three or four matches during the actual event, so there's lots of new-to-me games to get through each year. Then I'd watch, and pick a player. When they swept, I swept. So I could watch along with a game, try to learn some strategy, and also sweep at a realistic game cadence and duration (with a realistic rest period in-between bursts).

There are various options for setting up a dryland training platform if you don't happen to keep every "as seen on TV" gizmo ever made in a pile in your basement. For example, sports stores with hockey gear may sell "artificial ice" for hockey practice, some of which are designed for stick handling and some which claim you can even skate on them. Even if you can't get a full sweeping setup, just getting into the sweeping position can help build the arm and core strength to hold yourself up when you get back to the ice next season.

SOFT SKILLS

Curling is a team sport. Being a good team member is much more than being technically good at the elements of curling. There are a lot of important soft skills.

There's communication, on-ice and off-ice, sure. There's being a decent human being who can hang around and fit in with three other human beings, which is usually no problem at all but every now and then seems like a high bar. Other than pointing out that it's important, it's not something I can really teach.

There are a few general points to keep in mind. If you get to play with the same group of people in a team or league, you'll learn about how much everyone likes to joke around vs take things seriously, how open people are to feedback (or to teaching you), etc. When you're on a new team (whether because you're sparing or the league mixes things up), you may have to fall back on some general aspects of the positions' responsibilities to have the team function.

If you are sparing, then you are likely the odd one out on an otherwise (hopefully) functional team. So try to be flexible and work with the team the way they want to play.

As front end (Lead or Second) player, you're not the Skip, even if you have a decade more skipping experience than the current Skip. Let them learn, and find that balance where you can make the odd suggestion (especially if they have to adjust how much ice to give for your unique delivery), but don't call the game from the hack.

As Skip, adapt to your players: your usual team may want to play super defensively, but this team may be more interested in making draws. They may have different deliveries and releases than you're used to, so you may have to adjust how much ice you give or what kinds of shots you call.

And everyone needs to keep etiquette in mind. Each league will develop its own culture, but generally in curling we never applaud or cheer an opponent's miss, even if it sets it up nice for us. We will applaud and congratulate them on their good shots (or their unintended lucky outcomes) even when it costs us the game. And with spares, they may not know what you mean by a "board" hit, or what that thing the Skip is doing with her broom means, or what all the numbers the sweepers are yelling out means. Don't be afraid to ask, and also be understanding if someone needs help getting up to speed.

Matching personalities: Personality conflicts happen, regardless of skill level. Sometimes in leagues that pick

Potpourri

teams randomly or that rotate players, you may get stuck with someone you don't gel with – try to make it work for that short time period. But sometimes you're in a team for longer, and you may just find you keep butting heads with a certain someone – and that may be exclusively an on-ice phenomenon. Yes, I am saying that sometimes married couples make poor curling teammates and it's fine to play on separate teams (and says *absolutely nothing* about the off-ice relationship). Yes, I'll sweep with your wife* so you can play on separate teams.

VARIANT: DOUBLES

I'm an avid Mixed Doubles player and love this variant of curling.

As the name implies, it's played with just two players per team, typically one man one woman (often called "Open Doubles" for any two people). Each team delivers five rocks, with one player throwing first and last ("the bun") and one throwing the middle three ("the burger")†.

It is fast and athletic: you're usually calling your own shots, and sweeping your own rock (getting up to chase it after you let go, though that's not a requirement if you're not comfortable with that). With only two players you have to choose carefully whether you want someone holding the broom in the house calling line or a sweeper for each shot.

To help get things going, doubles starts with one rock for each team pre-positioned in play: the hammer team starts with one at the back of the 4', and the non-hammer

---

* I wish I could take credit, but the pun is a classic of the genre.
† I promise you I did not just make these terms up, but they are definitely not universally used. I haven't heard of a more common term for these positions yet though.

191

team starts with a guard on the centreline, mid-way up. Exactly how far "mid-way" is for the pre-positioned depends on how much the ice is curling, and is something the teams are supposed to agree to in advance. Your league or spiel may specify, but typically a spot (or several spots) is designated in the ice, perhaps with a painted hash mark or a coin frozen in place, and then the rock is placed on one side or the other of the spot. The idea is that the rock should be close enough to the house that it protects the pre-positioned stone from a hit, but allows enough space for a draw to the button to get by. So on ice that curls more, the pre-positioned guard would be placed closer to the house, on straighter ice the guard would be placed closer to the hog line. Once determined, the same spot is then used throughout the game.

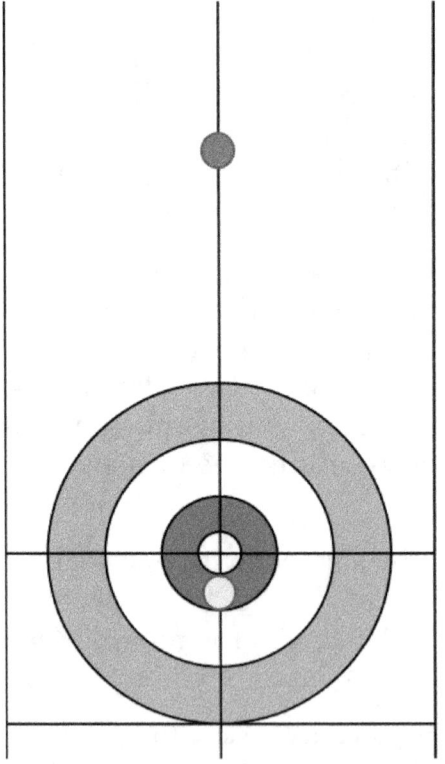

Guard: rock belonging to team that throws first, on the centreline. Depending on amount of curl, may position in front of or behind marker in ice

House: rock belonging to hammer team starts with back edge of rock touching edge of 4' circle

Then there is a "modified free-guard zone" – none of the first 5 rocks, including the two pre-positioned ones, can be removed from play (i.e., three thrown rocks before a hit can be made). So like four-person curling, it's the hammer team's second player that can throw the first hit. Unlike the free-guard zone in four-person play, it includes rocks in the house: no hits of any kind. It also doesn't have a "non-offending team" to make a decision – *no* rocks, *not even your own*, can be removed, and if they are there is no choice about it, they *must* be replaced as they were prior to the shot (though if you tick a rock but keep it in play, the *shooter* is allowed to roll out of play).

This encourages messy, complicated ends, as the first few rocks will typically be draws, guards, or gentle ticks.

There are even more quirks in store for doubles players: you're allowed to switch positions before each end, which may be for some strategic reason (e.g., you may want your stronger hitter throwing more rocks in the middle if you're aiming to keep the score down for an end, or you may want your better drawer throwing first if you're in a must-steal situation), or just to try to even out how many rocks each of you gets to throw in a game.

Blank ends switches which team gets hammer, which strongly discourages teams from playing toward a blank (it will always be better to take the force when you can). And technically, it's *choice* of hammer – if you prefer to throw first and try to steal (which the starting positions help make perhaps a bit more likely than the empty sheet of four-person curling), you may give the other team the hammer.

Yet another quirk is the "power play" – one end per team per game where you can change the location of the pre-positioned stones to start on one wing or the other (your rock in front of the T-line, splitting the 8' and 12', their rock as a guard that from a position on the centreline between the two hacks appears to be directly in front of yours). This setup should put the hammer team in a stronger position to score.

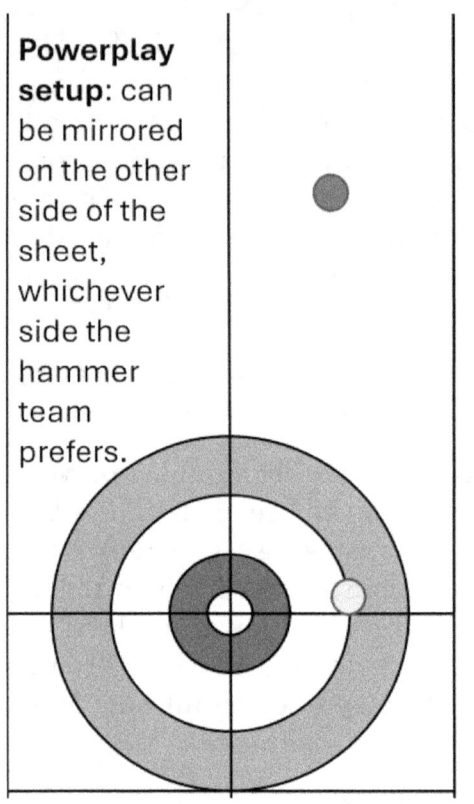

Powerplay setup: can be mirrored on the other side of the sheet, whichever side the hammer team prefers.

Guard: same distance from hogline as other ends, moved to the side. Perfectly in line with the stone in the house when viewed from between the two hacks.

House: rock belonging to hammer team starts with back edge of rock touching T-line, splitting 8' and 12' circles.

It's fast-paced, athletic, messy, and with only one other person on your team, so much is up to you. I personally love it, and encourage you to at least give it a whirl.

Some clubs dislike doubles leagues because it means there are half as many curlers on the ice: that can mean less bar revenue from broomstacking (though that largely depends on *which* half still show up for doubles – at our club the bar does not hurt on doubles nights) and fewer people paying for ice time. The flip side is that if you have a timeslot that's hard to fill, you can try a doubles timeslot and see if you can round up enough players that way. Because mixed doubles is faster, you may also be

Potpourri

able to squeeze an extra game in a timeslot that may not quite be long enough for an extra four-person game.

Power Play Tips

In players new to doubles, I commonly see a lot of confusion about what to even do with the power play. It's something you may not even encounter once per game (particularly in a doubles league with lots of other teams reticent to use it). Your tactics for it will depend on your goals.

As hammer team, you may want to use it to score at least two – you are trying to **generate offense**. In which case, you probably want to keep play going to the wings: put another rock behind your starting guard, or split the house by drawing to the other side (especially if the non-hammer team opened by ticking the guard). You can even put up another corner guard. The non-hammer team can't hit you until their third rock, so you get some opportunities to draw one or two more in for more offense.

You may also want to use it as a way to increase the odds of scoring *at least* one – you are going to use it **defensively**. In this case, you start with the middle open, and all you want to do is keep it that way so that you can draw one in with your last rock to get your single point (and keep the other team from scoring). If that's your aim, then odds are good that the other team is going to try to bring play back to the middle – they will likely either draw to the top of the house, or try to put a centre guard. If they succeed, you will not be allowed to *hit* it on your first shot... but you can *tick* it.

Indeed, a number of really strong power play responses involve moving rocks in play around during the modified free guard zone, which can be like playing with fire: raises and ticks are *hard*, and if you accidentally put a rock out of play (or miss and sail past the backline yourself), you've given up one of a very few number of rocks in the end and halted your momentum.

Anyway, to try to stay defensive if the non-hammer team starts with a rock near the top of the house on the centre, you can try to tick it. If you raise a top-house rock to the back, or tick a centre guard to a corner, you'll be in pretty good shape – you'll be allowed to hit everything thrown near the centre after that, and can do just that; if they play to the wings, well, that's what you wanted in the first place. If you fail the tick (typically by throwing too heavy or hitting a guard too thick), and knock their rock out of play, then it's not the end of the world: it gets put back, they get one more attempt to draw, and then you get to start hitting, and now you just have to manage a double (or for them to miss replacing the guard) in one of four attempts.

As the non-hammer team, you don't get to choose when the power play happens, so it's perhaps even more important to have a plan to defend against it. The typical approaches are to:

- Try to bring the play back to the middle, which helps position you to steal or force.
- Try to keep the score down. You may do this by trying to open with a freeze to the shot rock on the edge, or by trying to tick the starting guard.

Keeping the score down is fairly do-able. The tough part is trying to steal in a power play: that usually requires the hammer team to miss somewhere. Still, I've had plenty of teams steal on my power play so I can testify that it is entirely possible.

The tick on the starting guard is a tough shot: your shooter is permitted to roll out, but even then it's a narrow band of weights and lines to tick it somewhere useful. However, if you accomplish it, it can provide two benefits: opening the pre-positioned stone on the wings to be hit later, *and* bringing play back to the middle with one of your stones.

HAPPINESS AND THE ZEN OF CURLING

Big transitions are usually good times to stop and reflect: new year's, birthdays, and the end of the curling season. Did you get what you wanted out of this season? What do you want to get out of next season? Or at the beginning: what do you want out of the season?

That may involve taking a step back to frame the questions properly: how does curling fit into your life? What do you need to get out of curling to help complete your life?

Now for me, curling fills the void where I would otherwise have a personality. *Hi, I'm John, the curling nerd. Have you seen my collection of curling pun T-shirts?*

But more seriously, science has been trying to answer questions about how to live "well" – which means different things to different people – and there are many approaches to address that nebulous set of questions, and the good news is that with just a little bit of squinting, curling fits well into *all* of them. First off, to live happier, more fulfilled lives the PERMA model suggests that some of the things we should pursue include:

Positive emotion – like sharing smiles and laughs with teammates and opponents alike in a friendly game or chat afterwards.

Engagement – being in a "flow" state where you feel fully immersed in some activity. Sure writing a book is great, but there's nothing for flow like being mid-slide feeling like you're flying across the ice, the rumble of the rock parting the air in front of you.

Relationships – even introverts like me are supposed to talk to other people, and team sports help enable that without those awkward silences where we're expected to hold up our end of the conversation.

Meaning – serving your community does help you feel more contented in your life, which could be helping someone out with a spare request, giving your all to sweep your teammate's nearly hogged guard over the line, or volunteering for various activities at the club.

Accomplishment – advancing in your skills or pursuing mastery is the last factor, and you can work toward improving all kinds of skills in curling, from reading the ice to throwing to communication, and it's a subtle and tricky enough sport that even decades later there's still room to improve.

And maybe some or all of those elements will drive your goals for your curling year, whether it's to make new friends and build new relationships, strengthen your community, or work toward mastery of new skills.

Likewise, there's science behind healthy aging, another way to interpret what "living well" means. And even the 20-year-olds reading this *do* need to think about aging in a healthy way, because the sooner healthy habits become actual habits, the easier it will be to maintain them. Same for strength and flexibility: it is way easier to maintain than build. Let me tell you, as someone who went all-in on mental development in my 20's thinking my body was just a fleshy transport container for my brain and I could ignore its needs to study more, ***it's not***. Physical health goes hand-in-hand with mental health – indeed one of the best preventative measures we have for

Potpourri

strokes, pretty much all the dementias, and memory loss in general is physical activity.

There's a lot of overlap between the factors for healthy aging and happiness in life. Regular physical exercise and socializing with other people (again, *even for the introverts*, which feels like a mistake but isn't, I checked) are two of the largest factors. And hey, curling checks both those boxes in one convenient package. The evidence is a little more conflicted on how helpful it is to be regularly challenging your brain with strategy games, but just in case, curling provides that too.

Anyway, once again I'm taking the scenic route to the point, which is that there are many things you may want to get out of your time curling, only some of which may be even tangentially related to getting better at curling. Simply curling more may be the start and end of your goals for next year. Or you may want to spend time with friends and meet some new people, and the curling part is entirely incidental.

Regardless, I hope this book was helpful in finding happiness in curling and improving your game.

RESOURCES

There are lots of great resources out there for improving your game.

Stephanie Thompson's *Empowered Performance* business offers lots of material to help improve your fitness and effectiveness as a sweeper, from personalized one-on-one sessions to webinars to free articles and her podcast series. https://empoweredperformance.ca/

Lean Curling was set up by Jotham Sugden after I had already finished the first draft of the book, and looks to be building a collection of information on sweeping science. https://www.leancurling.com/

Dr. Glenn Paulley's site includes several articles on cutting-edge sweeping research and more. https://glennpaulley.ca/curling/blog/

Curling Canada has some information on the basics, including the rulebook. https://www.curling.ca/basics/

The Ontario Curling Council has a number of webinars each year, several of which have been archived. https://curlinginontario.ca/learn/occ-webinar-series/

Matt Bean's Curling Class has a paywalled online course to learn to curl (which is much of what this book just covered, but sometimes it's helpful to hear it from another voice and with videos). They also offer to do video analysis if you record yourself. The site has free resources too, including some drills and a "scenario generator" to create some scenarios to discuss strategies over. https://curlingclass.com/

The Chess on Ice YouTube channel has a number of videos on curling strategy basics. https://www.youtube.com/@chessonice

Jamie Sinclair has a number of fantastic learn-to-curl videos on her YouTube channel (Curl Up With Jamie). https://www.youtube.com/@CurlUpWithJamie

Doug Wilson & Mickey Pendergast run a Facebook Group called Daily Curling Puzzle that discusses various strategy scenarios and is a lot of fun. They distilled down some of the general strategic and tactical principles into a book that uses 50 of the puzzles titled *What's Your Call?* https://www.whatsyourcall.info/

Bill Tschirhart ran a blog (though it may not have been called that at the time) called *A Pane in the Glass*, which was then rolled up into a book by the same name that is now a little hard to find. Some of the articles have been archived in various places on the web, and he now has a podcast *also* called *A Pane in the Glass*. He also has a new blog, with several articles on practice drills and coaching. http://truenorthbill.blogspot.com/

Sean Turiff has a book with a similar scope to this one called *Curling: Steps to Success*. It came out in 2016 so just before the directional sweeping revolution. He devotes more of his page count to practice drills which makes it a good complement to this book.

John Cullen has a limited-series podcast with CBC called *Broomgate: A Curling Scandal* that goes into the history of modern broom heads, the development of directional sweeping, and the solution of using an agreed-upon fabric (WCF) for all brooms in major competitions.
https://www.cbc.ca/listen/cbc-podcasts/1427-broomgate-a-curling-scandal

META

A PARTING REQUEST: THREE FAVOURS

Dear reader: As we reach the end of our time together, I have three favours to ask of you.

One for the sport: Keep the best of the *Spirit of Curling*, and be the change for any parts of the culture that should be changed. Culture is just a bunch of humans coming together, and you are (or soon will be!) one of those curling humans. Make the sport, and the culture around it, not only one you want to be part of, but one *anyone* should *want* to be a part of. Live up to the ideals of the honour, kindness, and sportsmanship of the Spirit of Curling.

One for you: Treat your body like it belongs to someone you love. It's not *at all* covered in the book, but eat right and drink some water from time to time. Get some exercise – including curling! Never stop learning and keep working on yourself as a human… but also be careful not to hurt yourself. Ice is slippery (in the rink and more so on the wintry roads), take care out there.

One for me: Every YouTube video and podcast ends with a plea to "like and subscribe" these days, and for books that idea is even more important: **books live and die on word-of-mouth**. Without a healthy pile of 5-star reviews, it's hard for people to tell that this is a good read vs. some slapped-together piece of low-effort AI garbage. Without word-of-mouth people won't go looking for it in the first place. Now the *Spirit of Curling* says that if it's *not* good that I should pull it like a burned rock so *honest* reviews are important and I don't want any other kind –

but also remember how low the bar is for 5 stars these days. If it's not good, well, I can't honestly say my feelings *won't* be hurt, but as an author you have to at least publicly pretend to have thick skin – regardless, I'll survive. I'm thrilled you read it and cared enough to pan it. So please, tell your friends and teammates. Post it to your socials. Ask your local library to carry a copy.

ABOUT THE BOOK AND ACKNOWLEDGEMENTS

In 2023, the Unionville Curling Club agreed to launch a new league – Open Tag – meant to be a "development" league and a place where people of all experience levels could play, but in particular to provide a home for people fresh out of our learn-to-curl programs.

I was a big advocate for starting such a league, and agreed to manage it to get it up and running. It was individual entry, so people didn't have to know other curlers at the club to form a team. That also meant people could seamlessly join partway through a year so we could provide a home for new curlers coming out of learn-to-curl and they wouldn't have to wait until the next season started.

As part of making it a development league, I thought I would write a "short tip" each week. "Short" for me ended up being an average of 3 pages, and I joked at the end of the year that "if it felt like you've read a whole darn book worth of tips this season… it's because it's not too far off." Of course, some people prodded me to go the rest of the way and make it an *actual* book, and well, here we are.

The initial tips had more content specific to Unionville, such as where to sign up to be a spare, or talking about our other leagues, or local stores to buy equipment from. They also featured some very rough MS paint sketches from me (one of which I kept because it's cute). Part of getting the work publication-ready was to restructure it into something reasonably coherent (yes, even with a *potpourri* section) versus a tip-of-the-week collection, and shooting new photos and designing new figures that were a little cleaner.

This book has some new content on top of that, but over two-thirds of it is ripped right from those weekly emails.

I'm a big believer in testing and iteration, and this book was no different from my other projects that way. A huge thanks to my alpha and beta readers who provided valuable feedback to help point out parts that didn't make sense, parts that could be better, and just enough ego stroking to keep the project moving to completion.

Jamie Watt (formerly of Canada, now in Japan) and Sandi Martin (Ontario) helped read it from the perspective of people who had never curled before. Helen Fan (Ontario), Kelly Robertson (Ontario) and Amy Yu (Ontario) provided the perspective of new curlers. Christine Mok (Ontario, an "improver" with 5 years of curling experience) read it as a relatively new curler. Kelly Tooley (Ontario) ran the learning and development program at Unionville for many years, and provided valuable perspective as an experienced curler, coach, and teacher.

A special thanks to Stephanie Thompson, who was not able to review the completed book (if you line up the publication timeline with her Instagram/podcast announcements you'll see she had a very good reason), but who did participate in our Open Tag league as an expert sweeper and mentor. She also provided some feedback and inspiration for the original set of weekly tips. And finally a huge special thanks to my daughter Lauren, who inspires me to teach the next generation of curlers, and asks so many excellent questions.

ABOUT THE AUTHOR

John Robertson, PhD is a scientist, writer, teacher, curler, and massive fan of em-dashes. He graduated with his doctorate in Medical Biophysics from the University of Western Ontario in 2011, and spends his days as a science writer & editor for the University Health Network in Toronto. He spends his nights October–April at the Unionville Curling Club, and the rest of the year wishing there was curling while writing nonsense on the internet.

He specializes in explaining complex topics for regular people, in science, personal finance, and apparently now curling. He is the author of *The Value of Simple: A Practical Guide to Taking the Complexity Out of Investing* and teaches investing for Canadians online at course.valueofsimple.ca. He has been an invited speaker in investing, post-PhD careers, and scientific grant development at a number of venues including the University of Toronto, York University, and the Toronto Public Library.

He writes under the pen name of *Potato* at holypotato.net, his long-standing personal blog with a large focus on personal finance. Feel free to send him an email, john@curlingbeginners.ca.

He is an avid club curler, playing mixed doubles, four-person curling, and sparing whenever called upon. Despite starting in Little Rocks and having over two decades of experience as a curler, he still does not know what draw weight is tonight. He is an NCCP certified Club Coach (which for those unfamiliar with the system, is like, the lowest level of certification, but something). He is a volunteer with the Little Rocks program at Unionville Curling Club, and also runs the Open Tag league there.

ABOUT THE PHOTOGRAPHER

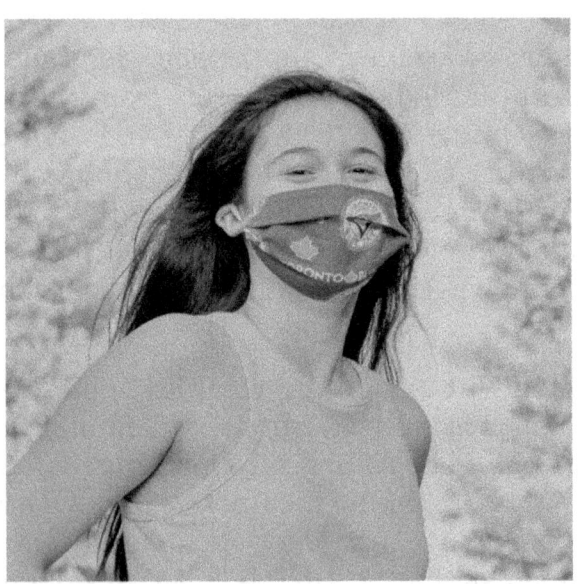

Alexis Lindley is a dynamic and passionate photographer from Canada. Raised in Markham, Ontario, Alexis was exposed to photography at a very young age and greatly influenced by her family. She is dedicated to her craft, specializing in capturing the profound emotions of athletes during sports events, the natural beauty of animals in their habitats, and the mood of stunning landscapes. Alexis's commitment to her art often drives her to explore new locations, seeking inspiration from the ever-changing landscapes that tell a unique story through each photograph.

Alexis started curling at a young age, and even as a junior (U18) curler was known around the Unionville Curling Club as a "super spare." She has played at the competitive level, including at the Ontario Mixed Doubles Provincial Qualifiers. She has helped tremendously with the club's operations, including photographing key events and helping to manage its social media presence.

For a deeper dive into Alexis' work, visit her Instagram page @angual.photography. There, you can explore more of her stunning photographs, which beautifully capture the essence of her passion for photography.

www.ingramcontent.com/pod-product-compliance
Lightning Source LLC
Chambersburg PA
CBHW071915290426
44110CB00013B/1370